KENT

KENT

FRAN & GEOFF DOEL

For Ken Thompson (1919-2001)
Man of Kent and Kentish Man

Originally published 2003
This edition published 2024

The History Press
97 St George's Place, Cheltenham,
Gloucestershire, GL50 3QB
www.thehistorypress.co.uk

© Fran and Geoff Doel, 2003, 2009, 2014, 2019, 2024

The right of Fran and Geoff Doel to be identified as the Authors of this work has been asserted in accordance with the Copyrights, Designs and Patents Act 1988.

All rights reserved. No part of this book may be reprinted or reproduced or utilised in any form or by any electronic, mechanical or other means, now known or hereafter invented, including photocopying and recording, or in any information storage or retrieval system, without the permission in writing from the Publishers.

British Library Cataloguing in Publication Data.
A catalogue record for this book is available from the British Library.

ISBN 978 1 80399 778 0

Typesetting and origination by The History Press.
Printed in Great Britain in TJ Books Limited, Padstow, Cornwall.

Trees for Life

CONTENTS

	Introduction	7
1	Spring & Summer Customs	13
2	Autumn & Winter Customs	31
3	Smuggling & Lore of the Sea	47
4	Hopping Down in Kent	59
5	Things Holy: Healing Saints, Holy Wells & Hermits	67
6	Pageants & Street Theatre	81
7	Things Unholy: Superstition & Witchcraft	93
8	Legends & Ghost Lore	101
9	Antisocial Customs	113
10	A Question of Charity	121
11	The Songs of the People	129
	Notes & Acknowledgements	139
	Appendix	145
	Bibliography	151
	Index	155

INTRODUCTION

'Kent, sir – everybody knows Kent – apples, cherries, hops and women', Mr Jingle says memorably in Charles Dickens' Pickwick Papers, a novel with a partly Kentish setting where Maidstone features as 'Muggletown' and Cob Tree Manor as 'Dingley Dell'. The Pickwickians and their host Mr Wardle like their food and a 'Kentish stomach' is traditionally a strong one. The Elizabethan poet Edmund Spenser also comments favourably on the women – 'Lythe as Lass of Kent' – and the traditional culture of fruit growing and hop picking is celebrated. What does Mr Jingle omit? Well, the plethora of Kent's indigenous saints and its former greatness as the most famous pilgrimage centre in Britain; the richness of its folk drama and rituals; and its maritime heritage of fishing, trade and smuggling to name but a few.

Kent is bounded on three sides by sea and has the longest coastline of any English county which, according to Parish and Shaw's *Dictionary of the Kentish Dialect*, contributed to the growth of a highly individualistic culture and in-breeding – hence the derogatory phrase 'Kentish Cousins':

> This county being two-thirds of it bounded by the sea and the river, the inhabitants thereof are kept at home more than they are in inland counties. This confinement naturally produces intermarriages amongst themselves.

Far from being insular, the maritime communities of Kent used the sea and rivers as mediums of travel and the Kentish ports thrived, not just as fishing communities rich in sea-produce (and sea-lore), but as trading centres with considerable traffic in people and goods and of significance in war as well as peace since Kent was usually the prime target for planned invasions. The Cinque Ports (four of which – Sandwich, Dover, New Romney and Hythe – are in Kent) had the responsibility under various charters of providing either fighting vessels or transports in times of war from late Anglo-Saxon times to the seventeenth century. This could be up to fifty-two ships for fourteen days in any one year in return for extensive privileges. Beyond the specified number of ships and days, an agreed payment was made.

These privileges included 'Den and Strond' – the right to haul boats onto the shore and to dry nets on the strand or beach – and exemption or reduction of certain import and export duties. The post of Lord Warden of the Cinque Ports (usually combined with the office of Constable of Dover Castle) was created to safeguard the rights of these ports and to reflect their influence in government circles. Remaining privileges today include holding Courts of Brotherhood and Guestling once a year and rights of attendance at coronations.

Since medieval times Sandwich has had a Mayor Deputy in each of its 'limbs' who send representatives annually for the ceremony of Confirmation of Deputies. For the privilege of links with Sandwich and its Cinque Port status, the towns are levied annual 'Ship Money' – 10s from Brightlingsea; 3s 4d from Fordwich; and 1s 8d from Sarre, which for many years has pleaded inability to pay at the ceremony for diverse ingenious reasons!

Proverbially Kentish miles were extra long, perhaps because of the vast breadth of the county (which seems to have been originally two distinct kingdoms and administrative areas surviving as East and West Kent, each with its bishopric) that gave rise to the proverb 'Essex stiles, Kentish miles, Norfolk wiles, many men beguiles'. Early division may have a bearing over the long controversy about the distinction between 'Men of Kent' and 'Kentish Men', neatly summed up by Alan Major in his *A New Dictionary of Kent Dialect*:

> Formerly 'A Man of Kent' was a man born between the Kentish Stour and the sea, all others being 'Kentish Men'. Another version said that a 'Kentish Man' was one born in Kent, but not of Kentish parents, while a 'Man of Kent' was

one whose parents and ancestors were Kentish. A more common version is that a 'Man of Kent' is one born east of the river Medway, while a 'Kentish Man' is one born west of the Medway.

Despite these apparent differences between East and West Kent, and affinities between West Kent and East Sussex (particularly with regard to folk songs and customs and smuggling and hop-picking traditions) there are distinctive features in Kent folklore, perhaps partly due to insularity caused by the bad roads through the rich and fertile Wealden clay, which gave rise to the proverb 'Bad for the Rider, Good for the Abider!'

Kent has always been important and wealthy; Julius Caesar commented on how civilised the Britons were in the south-east and the wealth of Kent is cited in early proverbs:

A Gentleman of Wales, with a Knight of Cales*
And a Lord of the North Countrie,
A Yeoman of Kent upon a rack's Rent
Will buy them out all three.

*A knight made by the Earl of Essex on his Cadiz expedition (1596)

Another proverb connects wealth and poverty to healthy and less healthy terrain in Kent:

Rye, Romney *and* Hythe, *for wealth without health;*
The Downs *for health with poverty;*
But you shall find both health and wealth
From Foreland Heath *to* Knole and Lee.

The first line refers to the area of Romney Marshe, the 'sixth continent', infamous for 'Kentish Ague', a kind of marsh fever. The marsh is one of several distinctive areas of Kent with their own economic, social and cultural traditions and terminology (such as the 'Romney Looker' meaning a shepherd). The Isle of Thanet is another and perhaps also are those former parts of Kent now sadly captured by Greater London (but which we shall nevertheless include in this book).

William Lambarde writes in his *Perambulation of Kent* that:

> The yeomanrie, or common people... is no where more free, and jolly, than in this shyre: for besides that they themselves say in a clayme (made by them in the time of king Edwarde the First) that the communaltie of Kent was never vanquished by the Conqueror, but yeelded itself by composition.

Lambarde and other early chroniclers cite the traditional story that by their threatened armed resistance the people of Kent persuaded William the Conqueror to allow them to continue with their ancient customs, one of which was inheritance under the Gavelkind system, which legally remained as the Common law of Kent until the twentieth century. Lambarde says that:

> Copyhold tenure is rare in Kent, and tenant right not heard of at all. But in place of these, the custome of Gavelkind prevailing every where every man is a freeholder, and hath some part of his own to live upon.

Alan Major defines Gavelkind as:

> An ancient Saxon custom distributing an equal division of the lands of the parent among his sons or children. From the Anglo-Saxon *gafol*, a tribute, although it has been suggested gavelkind is a corruption of the German *gieb alle kind* (give all to the children).

As Percy Maylam pointed out in his detailed pamphlet on the subject in 1913, Gavelkind remained the usual system of inheritance throughout the kingdom until at least the reign of Henry III, so we need to look for another reason for its long survival in Kent; Percy Maylam suggests this might be 'The small number of tenures in Kent held by knight service', that is military service as opposed to the 'non-military tenure of 'free scotage' or agricultural or monetary services.'

One of the advantages of Gavelkind was that if the father was executed for treason or other crimes, only his goods and chattels but not his land were forfeit to the crown, hence the Kent proverb:

> *The Father to the Bough, [the gallows]*
> *And the son to the Plough*

Earlier versions of this had 'logh' (meaning 'place') instead of 'plough'. Another distinct feature of Gavelkind rehearsed in a Kentish proverb was that the widow of a tenant was allowed to keep the estate if they were childless or their children under age. If any of the children were of age, the widow kept half the estate during her lifetime. The relevant proverb, found in its earliest form in the Queenborough Statute Book, runs: 'Si that is wedewe, si is levedi (She that is a widow, she is the lady).

Kent has had its fair share of political, religious and socio-economic rebellions and disturbances, with their own rich folklore and proverbial terms and sayings. 'Kentish Fire' for example was a term given to the continuous cheering common to the Protestant meetings held in Kent in 1828 and 1829 opposing the Catholic Relief Bill. The following proverb is a pithy reference to the social injustice of enclosures:

It is a fault in man or woman
To steal a goose from off a common.
But it admits of less excuse
To steal a common from a goose.

Kent's rich folklore has been inseparable from its traditional culture – its economic, social and religious way of life – which has included saints and smugglers, hoodeners and hop-pickers. Evolving patterns of life still affect living and developing folklore; for example for people standing in the middle of West Malling: 'If you can hear a train it's going to rain'. Will Kent folklore and customs ever cease to fascinate patriots and friends of this remarkable and historic county? 'It won't happen till the moon comes down in Calverley Road' as they say of impossibilities in Tunbridge Wells!

This book was originally written in 2003 and published by Tempus. The History Press then republished it in 2009 and reprinted it twice; this new edition for 2024 has a few additions, particularly enhancing the lesser known lore of East Kent (where the authors now live). We are grateful for the interest the book has stimulated over 20 years.

1

SPRING & SUMMER CUSTOMS

Traditionally, spring begins on St Valentine's Day (14 February) when the birds mate – 'the Birds' Wedding Day' as it was called in neighbouring Sussex. Geoffrey Chaucer, a poet with strong Kent connections, uses this tradition in his dream-vision poem 'The Parliament of Fowls' from around 1382:

> *For this was on seynt Valentynes day,*
> *Whan every foul cometh there to chese his make,*
> *Of every kynde that men thynke may*

That sexual pairing on this day extended to human beings, at least symbolically and traditionally, is shown by the final verse of the folksong 'Dame Durden', found extensively in the south of England including Kent and Sussex:

> *Twas on the morn of Valentine*
> *When birds began to prate,*
> *Dame Durden and her maids and men*
> *They altogether mate*

CHORUS
Twas Moll and Bet and Doll and Kit
And Dorothy Draggletail;
It was Tom and Dick and Joe and Jack
And Humphrey with his flail.
Then Tom kissed Molly
And Dick kissed Betty
And Joe kissed Dolly
And Jack kissed Kitty
And Humphrey with his flail
And Kitty she was a charming girl
To carry the milking pail

In Sussex the Copper family version bowdlerises the sexual word 'mate' to 'meet'.

In the seventeenth century there was a custom (operating among the middle classes at least) that the first man to greet a lady on St Valentine's Day would be her Valentine; husbands apparently didn't count! This involved the man buying the lady a present, such as a pair of gloves and some harmless social contact later in the day (such as sitting next to each other at a Valentine's Day feast); probably a kiss was also permitted. That the lady had to 'accept' the first comer, and therefore contrived to ensure the man was acceptable, is shown by the reference in *Samuel Pepys' Diary* for St Valentine's Day 1662:

> Valentine's day. I did this day purposely shun to be seen at Sir W. Battens – because I would not have his daughter to be my Valentine, as she was the last year, there being no great friendship between us now as formerly. This morning in comes W. Bowyer, who was my wife's Valentine, she having (at which I made good sport to myself) held her hands all the morning, that she might not see the paynters that were at work in gilding my chimney-piece and pictures in my dining-room.

Originally gifts were sent to one's Valentine; there are records of this happening in Roman society at this time of year and the festival, named after an early Christian martyr, may have absorbed features of some earlier celebration or ritual connected with springtime courtship. Love notes and cards became popular in the eighteenth and nineteenth centuries. Shakespeare has a hero called Valentine who serenades his love outside her bedroom window in *The Two Gentlemen of Verona* and in East Anglia there are records of children singing love songs outside houses on Valentine's Morn to collect pennies, which might be the remnants of an adult custom.

Shrovetide

Shrovetide is a moveable spring festival; the name derives from two Anglo-Saxon words meaning 'the time to be shriven' – to confess one's sins before the forty-day Lenten fast during which the consuming of meat, milk, eggs, butter and cheese were forbidden on weekdays. The 'shriving bell' (later known as the 'pancake bell' at Maidstone) summoned people to church in pre-Reformation days. After the service and shrivings there was the consumption of food forbidden in Lent incorporated into traditional pancakes to be used up and then the playing of rough sports such as street football and cock-fighting which were also frowned upon in Lent. The pancakes and violent sports survived the Reformation and there is a reference to the ringing of the pancake bell in Maidstone to encourage the wives to begin the repast. Taylor's 'Jack-a-Lent' (1630) includes a recipe:

> There is a thing called wheaten flowre, which the cookes doe mingle with water, eggs, spice and other tragicall, magicall inchantments, and they put it by little into a frying pan of boyling suet where it makes a confused dismall hissing (like the Learnean snakes in the reeds of Acheron, Stix, or Phlegeton), untill, at last by the skill of the Cooke, it is transformed into the forme of a Flap-jack, cal'd a pancake, which ominous incantation the ignorant people doe devoure very greedily.

At Olney in Buckinghamshire there is a famous Shrove Tuesday Pancake Race for the housewives, who toss pancakes in saucepans as they race, which has recently been copied by a local ladies' society in Tunbridge Wells. Shrovetide afternoon continued as a half-day holiday for schools into the nineteenth and twentieth centuries, with the tradition of 'barring out' the teacher, who was only admitted to the classroom on condition that he or she agreed to a half day holiday. Consequently all sorts of strange customs and sports are recorded on Shrove Tuesday afternoon such as this one, reported to the *Gentleman's Magazine* 'as occurring in an unspecified East Kent village' in 1779:

> I found an odd sort of sport going forward: the girls, from 18 to 5 or 6 years old, were assembled in a crowd, and burning an uncouth effigy, which they called an Holly-Boy, and which it seems they had stolen from the boys, who, in another part of the village, were assembled together, and burning what they called an Ivy-Girl, which they had stolen from the girls; all this ceremony was accompanied with loud huzzah, noise and acclamations. What it all means I cannot tell, although I inquired of several of the oldest people in the place, who could only answer that it had always been a sport at this season of the year.

Easter

Because of the significance of the Last Supper and the Maundy traditions (based on Christ's commands to his disciples to assist the poor), Easter was a favourite time for bequests giving annual doles to the poor. Kent's most famous Easter tradition, the Biddenden Dole, is covered in chapter 10. Egg rolling derives traditionally from north-west England, but in Tunbridge Wells eggs have been rolled on Easter Monday in the Calverley Gardens since the 1970s.

May Garlands

The first of May celebrates the beginning of summer in the traditional calendar with maypoles, may garlands and Jack-in-the-Greens. May Day was an unofficial bank holiday for many years and in the morning children used to carry May garlands from door to door, sometimes with a doll therein representing the May Queen, singing a song which included requests for the customary tribute and inappropriate religious reminders of man's mortality. The Whitstable May Song is typical in this bizarre mixture of celebration, begging and gnomic religious reflection:

> *The first of May is garland day, we wish you a merry May,*
> *We hope you like our May garland because it is May day.*
> *A branch of May we have brought you and at your door we stand,*
> *It is but a sprought, but well budded out by the work of our poor hands.*
>
> *This morning is the first of May, the primest of the year,*
> *So people all both great and small, we wish you a joyful year.*
> *We have been wandering all the night and almost all this day*
> *And now returning back again, we've brought you in the May.*
>
> *I have a purse upon my arm and drawn with a silken string.*
> *It only wants a few more pence to line it well within.*
> *Come give us a cup of your sweet cream, or a jug of your fine beer*
> *And if we live to tarry the town, we'll call another year.*
>
> *The life of man is but a span, he's cut down like the grass,*
> *But here's to the green leaf of the tree, as long as life shall last.*
> *So why not do as we have done the very first day of May?*
> *And from our parents we have come, to roam the woods so gay.*

And now we bid you all adieu and wish you all good cheer,
We'll call once more unto your house before another year.
God bless our Land with power and might, send peace by night and day.
God send us peace in England, and send us a joyful May.

In some areas in Kent, May Day was called Garland Day; the earliest reference we have to a procession carrying a May garland in Kent is in 1672, when one was ambushed by the press gang looking for recruits to fight the Dutch. Thomas Trowsdale wrote a detailed account of 'Garland Day' at Sevenoaks in 1880:

> This morning I had the pleasure of witnessing a lingering remnant of the olden observances of "Merrie May-day". Numbers of children went about from house to house in the Sevenoaks district in groups, each provided with tasteful little constructions which they called May-boughs and garlands. The former were small branches of fruit and other early blossoming trees secured to the end of short sticks, and were carried perpendicularly. One of these was borne by each of the children. Two in every group carried between them, suspended from a stick, the "May-garland", formed of two transverse willow hoops, decorated with a profusion of primrose and other flowers, and fresh green foliage... At every door the children halted and sang their May-day carol, in expectation of a small pecuniary reward from the occupants of the house... Middle-aged matrons who have resided in this part of the 'garden of England' all their lives, speak in terms of pardonable pride of the immense garlands of their girlhood. Forty years ago, I am told, the May-garlands often exceeded a yard in diameter, and were constructed in a most elaborate manner.

Another account of nineteenth-century garlanding comes from Bearsted:

> The custom of "garlanding" occupied the girls on May Day. They would dress a doll suitably for the occasion, and would then fix it to two garlanded hoops. The whole would be covered with a sheet, which was lifted for a small token to reveal the undoubted beauty of some of the creations of flowers.

A photo from around 1913 shows a May Day procession of infants at Hadlow School. A May Queen was chosen by votes by the children and was given a cross and chain by the wife of the vicar; other girls acted as attendants and dresses were kept at the school. The custom was recorded as late as 1933 and there was also Maypole Dancing.

The association of young girls with garlands has a sadder connotation in the widespread custom of 'virgin' or 'maiden's garlands' hung in church at the funerals of young unmarried girls. Such a garland was noticed at Plaxtol Church in 1836 – 'a garland and a pair of gloves cut in white paper hanging from the roof'. A letter to the *Gentleman's Magazine* in 1747 from a Bromley correspondent records the discovery of a garland by the parish clerk who:

> By his digging a grave in that church-yard, close to the east of the chancel wall, dug up one of these crowns, or garlands, which is most artificially wrought in filigree work with gold and silver wire, in resemblance of myrtle... whose leaves are fasten'd to hoops of larger wire of iron, now something corroded with rust, but both the gold and silver remains to this time very little different from its original splendour. It was also lined with cloth of silver.

Jack-in-the-Greens

Jack-in-the-Greens (men in wicker casings stuffed with evergreens) were sometimes known as the 'chimney-sweepers garlands', because the earliest accounts and drawings of them (from the late eighteenth and early nineteenth centuries) associate them with that occupation. The earliest surviving references are from London, but in the mid-nineteenth century many chimney sweeping families migrated to towns in the south-east, taking the custom with them. The tradition is documented in a number of Kentish towns, such as Lewisham, Deptford, Greenwich, Bromley and Orpington, and has been revived at Whitstable and Rochester. There is an eye-witness account of the Lewisham Jack-in-the-Green in 1894:

> May Day, 1894, at Lewisham. In the High Street, at the inn near St Mary's Church, we saw a Jack with a Queen of the May, two maidens-proper, one man dressed as a woman, and a man with a piano-organ. The organ was playing a quick tune and the Queen and the maidens danced round the Jack with a kind of "barn-dance", the Jack turning the other way. The man-woman sometimes danced with the maidens, turned wheels, and collected pence. The Jack was a bottle-shaped case covered with ivy leaves and surmounted by a crown of paper roses. The Queen wore a light-blue dress and had a crown similar to Jack's. The senior maiden wore a red skirt and a black body; the junior wore a white dress; each wore a wreath of roses. The man-woman wore a holland dress and over it a short sleeveless jacket; his face was blackened, and had a Zulu hat trimmed with red, the brim being turned up.

The Whitstable tradition of the Jack-in-the-Green on May Day survived until about 1912; a photograph of about 1910 survives, when a procession of morris dancers accompanied the Jack from outside the Duke of Cumberland, Horsebridge, to the site of the maypole. The Whitstable tradition has been successfully revived and moved to the early May bank holiday.

The well-known Rochester historian Edwin Harris witnessed the custom in his youth, and wrote two accounts, the first in a pamphlet published in 1899:

The first of May, the Sweeps used to perambulate the City of Rochester and district with a "Jack-in-the-Green" and collect money for a carousal. Also on the same day children from the country would carry garlands from door to door, soliciting money, with the usual phrase of "Please remember the Garlands".

In 1932, in one of a series of articles on *Recollections of Rochester* for the *Chatham, Rochester and Gillingham Observer* he gave a more substantial account:

There was a row of very old-fashioned cottages at the rear of the (Cock) tavern... The first of these cottages was inhabited by Mates, a sweep, from which circumstance it was sometimes called Sweep's alley... I have on several occasions seen the sweeps making their "green castle" there for the May-day festival of Jack-in-the-Green.

The "green" would be about six feet high, smaller at the top than at the bottom, which allowed the Jack to walk. On a level with his face was a small square aperture to enable him to see where he was going, also, incidentally, to admit of a quart pewter pot to be passed to him. At many of the public houses a pot or pots of beer would be given, and of this Jack would have his share, and as he danced and rotated as the party progressed, it was no wonder that he began to feel giddy and the green to wobble about in a strange manner.

On one occasion the morning of May Day was very bright, but also very cold. In the early evening the party returned with the green covered with snow; a snow-storm had started in the afternoon and was continuing as they returned.

Sixty years ago it was not considered May Day if we had not seen at least three Jacks-in-the-Green and their attendants from Rochester and Chatham.

SOOTY ATTENDANTS

Besides the Jack-in-the-Green there was always one man dressed somewhat like an Admiral, wearing white trousers and a crooked hat. He carried a long and large brass spoon, with which he collected the coppers. Several boys and young men in sooty clothes carried their copper shovels which they beat with their brushes, keeping time with the music, and at least half-a-dozen girls and young women dressed in short muslin frocks, like Columbines in a pantomime, and their hair adorned with flowers, would dance round and round the Jack-in-the-Green, beating tambourines in which they also collected coppers as opportunity occurred.

The band usually consisted of two men, one playing a violin and the other a big drum and the pandean pipes... The last of this band... was the wife of the master sweep in her Sunday-best clothes; she walked with the musicians and usually carried a shopping basket which had two flaps. As the money was collected, it was handed to her and a flap of the basket would be lifted and the coins dropped in. By the end of the day it became a weighty load to carry, as the contributions were mostly in coppers.

The author of *Dr Syn*, Russell Thorndike, in his biography of his sister Sybil (written in 1950) recalls a childhood memory of their time in Rochester where they were brought up:

Another fear we had was Jack-in-the-Green on May Day. Once, two of his mummers hoisted him over the wall, and he called out at us.

The Rochester celebrations were also on the first of May, but the popularity of its revival in the 1970s by Gordon Newton and the Motley morris (which included the rousing of the Jack from his winter slumbers in a nearby woodland at sunrise) has led to its expansion to the whole of the early May bank holiday weekend event entitled the 'Sweeps' Procession and May Festival'. The Jack is particularly featured in the Monday afternoon procession through the town, which usually starts from the Castle and features nearly 100 morris sides and groups of youngsters dressed up as 'climbing boys'.

Other Kent May Customs

The popularity of May garlands and Jacks-in-the-Greens may be connected to the banning of maypoles by Act of Parliament in 1644. Although maypoles were legalised again with the accession of Charles II, they never fully regained their earlier popularity. On May Day 1660, four weeks before the return of the King to England, Samuel Pepys was told 'how the people of Deale have set up two or three Maypoles and have hung up their flags upon the top of them'. Pepys also records in his diary that his wife went to bathe her face in May morning dew, which was said to be very good for the complexion. In the early sixteenth century, Catherine of Aragon and her ladies-in-waiting had done the same thing in Greenwich Park. Catherine and Henry VIII were treated to an elaborate May Day celebration at Shooters Hill in 1516:

> The King and the quene, accompanied with many lords and ladies, roade to the high grounde on Shooters hill to take the open ayre, and as they passed by the way they espied a company of tall yeomen, clothed all in grene, with grene hoods and bowes and arrowes, to the number of two hundred. Then one of them which called hymselfe Robyn Hode, came to the kyng, desyring him to see his men shote, and the kyng was content. Then he whistled, and all the two hundred archers shot and losed at once; and then he whisteled again, and they likewyse shot againe; their arrows whistled by craft of the head, so that the noyes was straunge and great, and muche pleased the kyng, the queen, and all the company. All these archers were of the kynges garde, and had thus appareled themselves to make solace to the kynge. Then Robyn Hood desyred the kyng and quene to come into the grene wood, and to see how the outlawes lyve. The king demaunded of the quened and her ladyes, if they durst adventure to go into the wood with so many outlawes. Then the quene said if it pleased hym, she was content. Then the hornes blewe tyll they came to the wood under Shooters Hill, and there was an arber made of bowes, with a hall, and a great-chamber, and an inner chamber, very well made and covered with floures and swete herbes, whiche the kyng muche praised. Then said Robyn Hood, Sir, outlaws' breakfast is venison, and therefore you must be content with such fare as we use. Then the kyng and the quene sate doune, and were served with venison and wine by Robyn Hood and his men, to their great contentacion. Then the kyng departed and his company, and Robyn Hood and his men them conducted; and as they were returnyng, there met with them two ladyes in a ryche chariot drawen with five horses, and every horse had his name on his head, and on every horse sat a lady with her name written... and in the chayre sate the lady May, accompanied with lady Flora, richly appareled; and they saluted the kynge with diverse goodly songs, and so brought hym to Grenewyche. At this maiying was a greate number of people to beholde, to their great solace and comfort.

Bringing maypoles and garlands into communities is an aspect of a wider tradition of decking houses with greenery on May Day of early derivation. In the 1420s the corporation of New Romney paid men from nearby Lydd 'when they came with their May'. Queen Elizabeth visited Sandwich in early May 1572, 'every house having a nombre of grene boughs standing against the dores and walls'. May Day was known as 'Flowering Day' in Tonbridge in the late eighteenth and early nineteenth centuries, when Head Boys from Tonbridge School collected flowers from neighbouring gardens to decorate the town and classrooms. On the 2nd or 3rd of May, Masters and Wardens of the Skinners Company (which endowed Tonbridge Public School) visited for a procession and church service and the High Street was decorated with birch boughs. An account of 1799 mentions a dozen old women from the nearby almshouses strewing flowers at the doorway of the school for the governors to walk over. In 1825 the date of this visitation was moved to July.

Morris Dancing

Morris dancing traditions are not as extensive for Kent as for other parts of the south of England but morris dancers are recorded as greeting Charles II in Kent on his return from exile. A parson in 1672 recorded that:

> Maidstone was formerly a very prophane town, insomuch that I have seen morrice dancing, cudgel playing, stoolball, cricket, and many other sports, openly and publicly on the Lord's day.

Sadly, no traditional morris steps survive from Kent, but a number of fine revival teams feature Cotswold morris dances. Stansted Morris originated in 1934 and metamorphosed into Hartley Morris in 1952, which is still going strong, celebrating its 50th anniversary in the year before the writing of this book. The Hartley morris men have an enormous repertoire of over a hundred dances and can be seen dancing outside of many of the most attractive and best ale pubs in West Kent on Thursday evenings in the summer.

Another highly respected Kent revival morris side, who danced in their heyday at the Sidmouth Folk Festival in 1987, was Mr Jorrocks. The team was formed on 1980 and their meeting and practice venue was the famous 'Bell and Jorrocks' Inn at Frittenden, itself a combination of the traditional name of the pub with the fictional Kentish character of Surtees' *Jorrocks, Jaunts and Jollities*. The distinctive high-stepping and jumping dance style (even including leapfrogs) of the side was based on the tradition of the Cotswold village of Oddington, near Stow-on-the-Wold, but Mr Jorrocks went even further back into the morris tradition by sometimes dancing to a pipe and a taborer, Helen Mitcham.

Rogationtide – Beating of the Bounds

A number of seasonal customs are perambulatory, including good-luck visitations round the community on a yearly basis. Beating of the Bounds is one of the most ancient, going back at least to Anglo-Saxon times, and it has a practical element, the preservation and memorising of local boundaries. The early Christian church may have been influenced by Roman culture in its institution of Rogationtide (which precedes Ascension Day, the 'Rogation Days' being the preceding Monday, Tuesday and Wednesday) for the ceremony of Beating the Bounds, for the Romans honoured a god of boundaries called Terminus and processed through the fields at the festival of *Ambarvalia* at the same time of year. In the English tradition, the parish boundaries were walked and the younger generation symbolically beaten or bumped to aid their territorial memories.

Some early Protestants viewed Beating of the Bounds with suspicion as another 'Romanish' concession to paganism, but Elizabeth I re-affirmed permission for clergy, churchwardens and parishioners to process on Ascension Day to define parish boundaries and offer up prayers for fruitful crops. The Diocese of Chichester in neighbouring Sussex, described their purpose in 1637 as 'knowing and distinguishing the bounds of the parishes, and for obtaining God's blessing upon the fruites of the ground'.

Photographs survive for early Beating of the Bounds ceremonies at Canterbury and Rochester, but the most interesting and humorous written account is of the Dartford Beating of the Bounds in 1850:

> Last Tuesday the "lower bounds", or "short bounds", as they are often called, probably from their being twice as long as the "upper" or "long" bounds of Dartford parish, were perambulated. The "Roman road" for a long distance was, of course, the bound mark so long as it could be adapted to that purpose. Humpings, immersions in the brooks, and other customary practices on these occasions were duly observed. As the boundary marks were more destroyed in this division than in the one perambulated the preceding week, a much longer time was occupied in the work before lunch-time. Certainly all parties were gratified beyond measure when the Long Reach tavern hove in sight... After luncheon the majority of the perambulators fancying their task was done, miraculously disappeared till dinner-time. Mr Landall and half-a-dozen other gentlemen, with the school-boys, started upon the work, and followed the Creek banks till they arrived at the spot where a boat was to have awaited them to cross the water to the opposite shore – for here, as Mr Dunkin shewed, great alterations had been made by the stream in its course since the days when the parishes were parcelled out. The old water-courses and old

embankments were however clearly defined; at the division of the water, however, there was no boat... the worthies gloomily trudged on more than two miles to a spot where the bottom appeared to be harder... Here Mr Landall and some others determined upon crossing, as a labourer offered to carry persons over the ford for a gratuity without wetting them. After much labour, and getting covered with tenacious mud, Mr Landall safely got, Friar Tuck fashion, upon the man's shoulders, but alas, after four or five steps, both tumbled down into the stream and were thoroughly soused, amidst the laughter of those on terra firma... The perambulators then tramped more than ten miles, all the way back and afterwards again crossed the Creek. At 8 o'clock, sadly jaded and muddy, shorn of banners and followers, the three gentlemen and the boy arrived at the primal bound mark, in Maiden-lane, from which they had started, and just contrived to bump the individual who had at the commencement of the perambulation received a similar favour, amidst the acclamations of a vast crowd.

Schoolboys are mentioned in this account, but no women. With the amount of uncertainties and things going wrong, one wonders if this was a revival of a custom rather than a regular event.

The Gillingham bounds were beaten in September 1932, the first time for eight years. They started at the dockyard 'where boundary stone No. 1 is situated near the water's edge beyond the Engine House and directly opposite Upnor Castle.' The stone was beaten with hazel sticks and celebrities were 'bumped'; the last stone was at Otterham Quay.

William Lambarde in his *A Perambulation of Kent*, mentions a skirmish between the monks of Rochester Cathedral and the brethren of Strood Hospital that took place in the time of Edward I, which sounds as of it might be caused by a Rogationtide or beating the bounds custom. The monks of Rochester undertook a procession 'to pray to God for raine' during a time of high wind and drought. Processing with banners and lighted candles and chanting Latin litanies, they took a short cut through the orchard of Stroud (Strood?) Hospital (having first obtained permission from the master). Because there had been 'great heats' between the two communities, the master chose not to inform the Hospital brethren of the Cathedral monks' right of access. Taking the law into their own hands, the Hospital brothers ambushed the Rochester monks in the orchard, attacking them with 'clubbes and battes'. The latter only escaped when one of their number ran hard against the locked postern door of the orchard causing it to burst open, 'and so both escaped himselfe, and made the way for the rest of his fellowes'. Lambarde suggests that 'The Frendsburie Clubbe Procession' grew out of this:

> They of Frendsburie used to come yeerely... upon Whitsonmondaie to Rochester, in procession with their Clubs, for penance of their fault.
>
> Lambarde, p.331

In the twentieth century, new or revived Rogationtide beating the bounds customs include the Blessing of the Fields at Hever and the Blessing of the Cherry Orchards at Newington. The Mayor of Rochester beats the bounds of his territory as Admiral of the River Medway between Garrison Point and Hawkwood by boat.

Oak Apple Day

Oak Apple Day (29 May) was originally a public festival, including a morning church service, to celebrate the restoration of the monarchy in 1660 and Prince Charles' safe concealment in an oak tree after his defeat at the Battle of Boscobel. Royalists wore sprays of oak or sycamore and Puritans and their sympathisers were liable to be beaten with nettles. When King George III reviewed troops at Coxheath in 1778, many male bystanders wore cockades of twigs of oak in their hats. In 1799 King George reviewed volunteer soldiers against the Bonaparte threat at the Mote Park, Maidstone, and members of the Cabinet wore sprigs of oak and the Queen and the royal princes wore oak; local shopkeepers decorated their premises with oaken boughs.

Friendly Societies and Club Walking

In the nineteenth century club walking was a feature of midsummer. These were the annual celebratory processions of the Friendly Societies and Benefit clubs, to which members made regular small monetary contributions as insurance against sickness, unemployment and death. For the annual 'Walk', club members dressed in their best clothes and paraded through town and village, often to the sound of a local band. The walk was usually followed by a church service and a feast.

Blessing the Sea & Whitstable Grottos

In coastal areas of Kent it was the sea, as the main provider, which was blessed. There are blessing of the sea festivals at Folkestone (on the Sunday following St Peter's Day at the end of June – 3 p.m. at the harbour) and

Whitstable in July where the oyster boats are blessed on St James's Day (25 July) in a ceremony dating back to at least the nineteenth century. Those who eat oysters on St James's Day in Kent are said to never be in need of money for the following year (St James, a fisherman, was patron saint of the Whitstable oystermen). A Kentish recipe for the eating of oysters is given in Brian Day's *A Chronicle of Folk Customs*, 'Serve plain on the deep shell, in their own liquor. Accompany with brown bread and butter, lemon wedges and wine vinegar, and serve a dry white wine or stout.'

The intriguing and picturesque custom of building grottos of oyster shells at Whitstable must also be a ritual connected with the oyster fishing season. A.O. Collard has the following description and explanation in *The Oyster and Dredgers of Whitstable* (1902):

> The children... find a use for some [oyster shells] in the construction of grottoes, which they illuminate at night with a piece of candle, generally on the first of August. Probably few people remember the origin of the old street petition, "Please remember the grotter!" The children who give utterance to it do so without much reference to its appropriate day, which should really be the Festival of St James, on 25 July. The legend runs that when the remains of that holy man were being brought from Palestine to Spain, of which country he was the patron saint, a knight and his horse fell overboard. The knight was saved without his horse, and on being rescued, the knight's clothes were covered with clinging oysters. This miracle, associated with the presence of the body of the saint, was the origin of the oyster grotto.

Robert Goodsall, who witnessed the custom in the early twentieth century, confirms the details and adds that the grottos were prevalent in the Horsebridge area and may also have featured on Guy Fawkes Night.

Joan Rootes in her article 'Only a Ha'penny Please' describes the custom in Margate in the early 1930s where 'children would gather together anything small and colourful – stones, shells, broken glass, crêpe paper, cigarette cards' and add moss and flowers and construct 'a picture inside a square about a yard each way'. Alternatively children would draw larger pictures on the sands, 'edged with chalk, shells or stones' and chant:

> *Please, spare a copper*
> *For my grotter,*
> *Only a ha'penny, please.*

The custom generally died out by about 1960, but there have been revivals, notably one organised for young holidaymakers by Margate Chamber of Commerce in 1979.

On an early Saturday in July the Admiralty Court of the City of Rochester has a meeting on the Medway near Rochester Pier in their regalia barge to regulate the oyster fisheries in the River Medway according to an Act of Parliament of 1729, and to swear in new Bailiffs for the year.

Harvest and Gleaning

John Brand in his *Observations on the Popular Antiquities of Great Britain* notes that Kent had a harvest tradition of the last sheaf (documented more recently in neighbouring Sussex) and that the Kentish term for a corn dolly was 'ivy girl' – which may shed some light on the curious Shrovetide custom cited earlier in this chapter.

Gleaning the remnants of the harvest was another customary rite, and one given sanction by Ruth in the Bible. *The Bearsted School Record Book* of 1876 mentions it as affecting attendance. In *A History of Bearsted and Thurnham* we are told that:

> The village people would collect as much as they could when the fields were thrown open for gleaners and would take it to the mill in Otham Lane. The charge for grinding was low and the flour would make several weeks' bread in their own houses.

Charlton Horn Fair

Prominent and notorious amongst Kent fairs, and certainly the one with the richest folklore, was Charlton Horn Fair, held on St Luke's Day (18 October), banned in 1872 for licentious conduct and recently revived. The wearing of horns was anciently a power symbol – even possibly originally a religious and fertility symbol – but by Shakespeare's day the wearing of horns clearly had a sexual connotation connected to cuckoldry. Broadsheets advertising the Horn Fair in the British Library show horned men and devils and one from the early nineteenth century prints the following rhyme:

> *Ye Hornifi'd Husbands who come once a Year,*
> *With Baskets, Pickaxes, and Spades to HORN-FAIR.*
> *To level a Path for your Waggish-taild Wives,*
> *If e'er you expect to lead peaceable Lives*

Make the best of your Bargains, and think it no scorn
That Fortune has doom'd you to wearing the Horn,
For 'twas worn by OLD NICK, before you were begotten
And will be so, after you're all dead and rotten,
Make him but yr Captain to fight for your Cause
And then you'll have nothing to fear, my brave Boys.

The 'Horn Fair Song' collected by Vaughan Williams from Frederick Teal at Kingsfold, West Sussex, is further evidence for the wearing of horns. Puzzlingly this song mentions a spring date and may not refer to Charlton Horn Fair. There is an Ebernoe Horn Fair in Sussex, but that is in July. Stray references in records in Kent and elsewhere suggest either a number of horn fairs and/or a symbolic or legalistic use of the term; J.R. Chanter in a nineteenth-century article on Devon customs mentions the nailing of horns to a church door as a claim to hold a cattle market as being described as 'horn fair'.

As I was a-walking one morning in Spring,
So soft blew the winds and the leaves growing green;
I met a pretty damsel on a grey mare,
As she was a-riding on to Horn Fair.

I asked this pretty damsel for to let me ride.
"O no", then: "O no, my mammy would sigh:
And besides my old daddy would bid me for sure
And never let me ride on the grey mare any more.

I can find by your talk you're for one game of play
But you will not ride me nor my grey mare today:
You will rumple my muslin and uncurl my hair
And I shouldn't be fit to be seen when I get to Horn Fair."

"O, O my pretty damsel, how can you say so,
Since it is my intention Horn Fair to go?
We will join the best of company when we do get there
With horns on our heads as fine as our hair."

There were the finest of horns as ever you did behold,
There were the finest horns as were gilded with gold;
And ride merrily, merrily, Horn Fair we did go
Like jolly brisk couples, boys, and all in a row.

Another possible link between ancient and modern is that the scandalous cross-dressing which occurred at the Fair is also a primitive symbol of fertility. A more Christian explanation for the horn imagery could be that the Fair was moved to 18 October by the early seventeenth century as this was the day of St Luke whose symbol was a bull.

The traditional story for the founding of Charlton Horn Fair and the reason for the wearing of horns, is that King John gave land and permission for the fair in compensation to a local miller whose wife he seduced. This apocryphal story perhaps reflects the perception of the goings-on at the fair – as do local names such as 'Cuckold's Point' (which might derive from the story). In reality, the Abbot of Bermondsey was granted a charter for an annual fair at Charlton in 1283. Philipot's *Villiare Cantianum* (1659) says that the name derives from 'the plenty of Winding-Horns, and cups, and other vessels of horn, there brought to be sold'.

Until the late eighteenth century a horned procession with a King and a Queen went from Bishopsgate to Rotherhithe and thence to Charlton to open the Charlton Fair, circling Charlton Church three times and attending a service there. In 1700 the fair was described as 'a sanctuary for ill-manners, a protection for all rudeness, an encouragement of wickedness, a revelling of young libertines, a looking glass of confusions, hurtful to all good manners and hateful to all good men.' Francis Grose in 1788 described the custom as:

> a riotous mob, who… meet at Cuckold's Point, near Deptford, and march from thence in procession, through the town and Greenwich, to Charlton, with horns of different kinds upon their heads, and at the fair… even the gingerbread figures have horns.

St Bartholomew Day (24 August), is celebrated at St Bartholomew's Chapel, Sandwich. The festivities begin with a ceremony, starting at 11a.m., and are followed by the Sandwich Bartlemass Bun Run at noon, when children run around the outside of the church and then are given a currant bun. Adults present are given a biscuit specially baked for the occasion, which has a marked date of 1190. The Chapel and Almshouses (still in use for 16 residents) are said to have been built to celebrate the defeat of the French in the thirteenth century.

2

AUTUMN & WINTER CUSTOMS

The hiring fairs of Michaelmas Day, (11 October, old style dating), is an appropriate beginning for autumn customs. In Kent farm labourers would sometimes carry a thin peeled 'shining stick', to symbolise their quest for employment.

Bonfire Night

Neighbouring Sussex has a plethora of bonfire societies which set the autumn and early winter ablaze, but in Kent only the West Kent village of Edenbridge can compete with a spectacular fire festival on the nearest Saturday to Guy Fawkes night, with a torch-lit procession featuring giant effigies of local celebrities such as Anne Boleyn and General Wolfe followed by a huge bonfire and fireworks. Pyrotechnist and fine traditional singer Dave Watts is the authority on the Edenbridge custom, which he researched and organised for many years, writing an illuminating article on it in the magazine *Fireworks* in 1985. Dave mentions that 'It was always the aim of the bonfire revellers to light their main conflagration in the middle of the bridge' and he discovered regular records on the eighteenth century in the

Edenbridge Parish Registers – 'Paid for guarding the bridge at Gunpowder Treason 10/-'. In 1709 the huge sum of £3 15s 2d was spent on 'liquor for the guards'. There is also a record of 'lighted barrels with turpentine balls' being rolled and fireworks let off in 1886.

The growth of bonfire societies to regulate the celebrations reflects civic concern at the often disorderly celebrations in the nineteenth century which descended from official instructions to celebrate the preservation of King James from the Gunpowder Plot in 1605. The date was conveniently close to that of the old Hallowe'en fires which burnt in Catholic times in many parts of the kingdom, but apart from this legacy of bonfires traditional Hallowe'en practices are not reported as surviving in Kent, though a number have been imported in recent years through Scots, Irish and Welsh settlers in Kent and through the influence of the commercialisation of the American Hallowe'en.

Local accounts and memories scattered throughout Kent suggest a nineteenth-century Guy Fawkes scenario as lively as Sussex in some areas, with processions, tar-barrels and effigies. In Plaxtol for example, the nineteenth-century young boys 'on Guy Fawkes Night would fix a long rod through an empty tar barrel, set light to it and roll it flaming down the street' and the historian of Bearsted School describes the lively celebrations on Bearsted Green:

> On Guy Fawkes' day, the Green was the centre of activities, and a huge combustible stack [was built] in the centre, while fireworks had been in construction for weeks in the place where the Railway Station now stands. The procession would march from the 'Bell' to the 'White Horse', people coming in from all directions and dressing in all kinds of appropriate costumes for the occasion. The central part of the procession would be a wagon bearing an effigy, the people lending an added touch of humour to the proceedings by shaping him in the likeness of whatever local figure seemed appropriate in that particular year. Mr Knowles (a local builder) once figured on the wagon as 'Tiger Knowles' and even the vicar himself provided the centre piece on one occasion under the name of 'Holy Joe'! Once on the Green, the fun started. With the effigy well alight and fireworks spluttering, flaming tar-barrels would be set going, and as the Green was very crowded, the excitement can be imagined.

Another traditional November festival which might have had some interrelationship with the developing iconography of Guy Fawkes Night, as it had effigies and fireworks, was Old Clem's Night – held in honour of St Clement, patron saint of blacksmiths, on his festal day of 23 November. Effigies of 'Old Clem' were paraded, anvils were fired and there were fireworks and songs – a favourite being the royalist blacksmiths' song, 'Twankydillo':

Here's a health to King Charlie and likewise his Queen,
And to all the royal family wherever they're seen,
Which makes my bright hammer to rise and to fall,
Here's to old cole and to young cole and to old cole of all.

E.P. Thompson, in his book *Customs in Common*, remarks on the decline of Old Clem and other trade-related customs in the nineteenth century, partly on account of rowdiness and the bourgeois attitude to this, and cites the complaint of a Woolwich shopkeeper that on St Clement's Day 1837: 'a procession got up by the Blacksmiths' apprentices passed through the principal streets of the town, attended by a large Mob, some carrying torches, others discharging fireworks in great abundance in the most reckless manner.'

Apple Wassailing

The traditional Christmas in Kent, however, has survived strongly, both in its specifically Christian aspect and in the Midwinter celebrations linked to the turning of the year with its practices of sympathetic magic. A good example of the latter is the custom of apple wassailing or 'howling', whereby a libation of cider punch was given to a representative cider apple tree in early January to invoke a bountiful crop of cider apples in the orchard the following autumn. The earliest known reference to this custom comes from Kent – from the village of Fordwich near Canterbury in 1595 to be precise. Two centuries later Edward Hasted describes the custom in his *History and Topographical Survey of the County of Kent* (1797-1801), though puzzlingly placing it during Rogation week:

> There is an odd custom used in these parts, about Keston and Wickham, in Rogation week; at which time a number of young men meet together with a most hideous noise, run into the orchards, and incircling each tree pronounce these words:
>
> *Stand fast root, bear well top;*
> *God send us a YOULING sop!*
> *E'ry twig, apple big;*
> *E'ry bough, apple enow!'*
>
> For which incantation the confused rabble expect a gratuity in money, or drink, which is no less welcome. But if they are disappointed of both, they, with great solemnity anathematise the owners and trees, with altogether as insignificant a curse.

> It seems highly probable that this custom has arisen from the antient one of perambulation among the heathens, when they made their prayers to the god, for the use and blessings of the fruits coming up, with thanksgivings for those of the preceding year. And as the heathen supplicated Eolus, god of the winds, for his favourable blasts; so in this custom, they still retain his name... this ceremony being called 'Youling', and the word is often used in their invocation.

Typically, as a Classicisist of the period, Hasted invokes the classical wind-god, but 'Youling' is much more likely to be derived from the Anglo-Saxon and Scandinavian name of 'Yule' for the Midwinter feast and this further confirms the midwinter, sympathetic magic and likely early origins of the custom.

The surviving words of the 'Blean Hoodening Song' sung around the parish of Blean, near Canterbury, on Christmas Eve, suggests a tradition of apple wassailing in East Kent as well, perhaps linked with the distinctive East Kent tradition of the Hooden Horse:

> *Three jolly hoodening boys*
> *Lately come from town*
> *Apples or for money*
> *We search the country round;*
> *Hats full, caps full,*
> *Half bushel baskets full –*
> *What you please to give us*
> *Happy we shall be.*
> *God bless every poor man*
> *Who's got an apple tree.*

The term 'wassailing' derives from the Anglo-Saxon words *waes hail* (be healthy) and a famous Kent legend, first recorded by Geoffrey of Monmouth in his *History of the Kings of Britain* (around 1136), tells how Reinwin, daughter of the fifth-century Germanic leader Hengist, greets the British leader Vortigern, who falls in love with her and marries her, disinheriting his children and causing civil war, with a toast wassail at a banquet. The story is repeated by later Kent writers such as William Lambarde in his *Perambulation of Kent* and in the Kent tradition the lady becomes known as Rowena. Although in Kent, with its prolific cider orchards, apple wassailing predominated, there was also a general midwinter/Christmas custom of wassailing in which seasonal toasts of mulled wine, spiced ale or cider were drunk from a wassail bowl at feasts or in house-to-house visitations by bands of wassailers, probably the originators of perambulatory carol singers. Surviving wassailing songs are not specifically religious, but invoke good health on visitants and visitors. A typical wassail song collected from neighbouring Sussex has the refrain, 'And may joy come to you and to our wassail'.

We have not discovered any evidence for the custom surviving the First World War in Kent, but there have been a number of revivals, notably the Chanctonbury Morris Men wassailing the apple trees at Tenterden in the 1970s and the Tonbridge Mummers and Hoodeners blessing the apple trees on New Year's Day at Cob Tree in the 1990s. Since the original publication of this book, Dave Hicks, along with the Ravensbourne Morris group, has made apple wassailing a regular early January ritual at various venues in the Keston area.

The Hooden Horse

Throughout Britain, animal disguise customs feature extensively in the Midwinter calendar, the most prominent involving horse disguise. The Kent variant is given the name of 'hoodening', of unknown derivation, but possibly denoting disguised or hooded. The tradition is documented in East Kent, particularly on the Isle of Thanet and usually involved the carrying of a wooden horse's head (as in Dorset and unlike the skull used in Cheshire, South Wales, Yorkshire, Derbyshire and Nottinghamshire). The earliest accounts, such as a letter of 1807 to *The European Magazine*, do however mention 'the head of a dead horse',

> Also at Ramsgate, in Kent, I found they begin the festivities of Christmas by a curious procession: a party of young people procure the head of a dead horse, which is affixed to a pole about ten feet in length; a string is affixed to the lower jaw; a horse-cloth is also attached to the whole, under which one of the party gets, and by frequently pulling the string, keeps up a loud snapping noise, and is accompanied by the rest of the party, grotesquely habited, with handbells; they thus proceed from house to house, ringing their bells, and singing carols and songs; they are commonly gratified with beer and cake, or perhaps with money. This is called, provincially, a Hodening, and the figure above described a Hoden, or Woden horse.

This is a further example, like wassailing, of a seasonal good luck visitation and perambulatory custom with ritual performances at a set time of year which are informally rewarded by the spectators or houses visited, thus binding performers and spectators into an act of sympathetic magic invoking good luck for the ensuing year. The letter's reference to a 'woden' horse as an alternative to 'hoden' or 'hooden' has fuelled speculation of a possible Anglo-Saxon pagan origin to the cult (as also in the case of 'wassailing'), particularly as Thanet is the region said by early chroniclers such as Bede (731), Nennius (early ninth century) and Geoffrey of Monmouth (around 1136) to have been allocated to the Germanic chieftains Hengist and Horsa, whose names mean 'stallion' and 'mare' and who are said by Bede to have descended from the Germanic god Woden. An adult folk custom such as dressing up as an animal is unlikely to have originated in the eighteenth century, and the wide provenance of these, plus the male-only participation and elements such as the cross-dressing and sweeper figure(s) in some of the accounts, suggest a development from a substantially earlier ritual.

Some accounts mention that it was the carters and stable lads who were involved in the tradition of 'hoodening' in the eighteenth and nineteenth centuries. There was a tradition of bleeding and resting the Kent farm horses over the Twelve Days of Christmas in preparation for the January ploughing and this would give the hands who worked with the horses some spare time for some fun and to obtain money or free drink through the custom. Perhaps the most graphic account comes from such a participant, writing to *The Church Times* in 1891 about his involvement in the custom in the 1840s:

> When I was a lad, about 45 years since, it was always the custom on Christmas Eve with the male farm-servants from every farm in our parish of Hoath and neighbouring parishes of Herne and Chislet, to go round in the evening from house to house with the Hoodining Horse, which consisted of the imitation of a horse's head made of wood, life-size, fixed on a stick about the length of a broom handle; the lower jaw of the head was made to open with hinges, a hole was made through the roof of the mouth, then another through the forehead coming out by the throat, through this was passed a cord attached to the lower jaw, which when pulled by the cord at the throat caused it to close and open; on the lower jaw large-headed hob-nails were driven in to form the teeth. The strongest of the lads was selected for the horse; he stooped and made as long a back as he could, supporting himself with the stick carrying the head; then he was covered with a horse cloth, and one of his companions mounted his back. The horse had a bridle and reins. Then commenced the kicking, rearing, jumping, etc, and the banging together of the teeth. As soon as the doors were opened the 'horse' would pull his string incessantly, and the noise made can be better imagined than described. I confess that in my very young days I was horrified at the approach of the hoodining horse, but as I grew older I used to go round with them... There was no singing going on with the hoodining horse, and the party was strictly confined to the young men who went with the horses on the farms. I have seen some of the wooden heads carved out quite hollow in the throat part, and two holes bored through the forehead to form the eyes. The lad who played the horse would hold a

lighted candle in the hollow, and you can imagine how horrible it was to one who opened the door to see such a thing close to his eyes.

Percy Maylam, a Canterbury solicitor, wrote the classic book on the Hooden Horse in a limited numbered edition in 1909; he first encountered the Hooden Horse whilst spending Christmases with his uncle at Gore Street, Monkton, from 1888-92:

> Anyone who has spent a Christmas in a farm-house in Thanet – it has been my good fortune to spend five – will not forget Christmas Eve; when seated round the fire, one hears the banging of gates and tramping of feet on the gravel paths outside (or, if the weather be seasonable, the more cheerful crunching of crisp snow), and the sound of loud clapping. Everybody springs up saying, 'The hoodeners have come, let us go and see the fun'. The front door is flung open, and there they all are outside, the 'Waggoner' cracking his whip and the leading the Horse (the man who plays this part is called the 'hoodener'), which assumes a most restive manner, champing his teeth, and rearing and plunging, and doing his best to unseat the 'Rider', who tries to mount him, while the 'Waggoner' shouts 'whoa'! and snatches at the bridle. 'Mollie' is there also! She is a lad dressed up in woman's clothes and vigorously sweeps the ground behind the horse with a birch broom. There are generally two or three other performers besides, who play the concertina, tambourine or instruments of that kind. This performance goes on for some time, and such of the spectators as wish to do so, try to mount and ride the horse, but with poor success. All sorts of antics take place, Mollie has been known to stand on her head, exhibiting nothing more alarming in the way of lingerie than a pair of hobnail boots with the appropriate setting of corduroy trousers. Beer and largesse are dispensed and the performers go further. Singing of songs and carols is not usually a part of the performance and no set words are spoken. In Thanet, occasionally, but not always, the performers, or some of them, blacken their faces. Years ago, smock frocks were the regulation dress of the party.
>
> In a house which possesses a large hall, the performers are often invited inside; at times the horse uses little ceremony, and opening the door, walks in uninvited.

Feeling that the Hooden Horse was becoming an endangered species in the Edwardian period, Percy Maylam researched at first hand and photographed the Hoodeners of St Nicholas-at-Wade in 1905, Walmer in 1906 and Deal in 1907, as well as doing extensive research in newspaper archives for his book. His accounts of the three teams are accurately observed as to both the details of the enactments, the Hooden Horses themselves and the sociological background of the custom and his book is a very enlightened piece of Edwardian folk research.

Sadly Maylam's fears for the immediate future of the Hooden Horse were realised. In the short term his own interest helped to stimulate revival of the St Nicholas-at-Wade tradition, including the re-introduction of the Mollie and besom broom for his photographs. However, the First World War effectively ended the tradition, although there was a brief survival at Deal in the early years after the First World War, as shown by a letter we received from Naomi Wiffen of Edenbridge in the early 1980s, who had lived in Deal as a child:

> I remember as a child being taken out on Christmas Eve to the High Street in Deal where the shops would be open very late, and it was the only time Deal children were allowed out in the evening, as parents were very strict. As we would be looking at the lighted shops, and listening to the people selling their wares, a horrible growl, and a long horse's face would appear, resting on our shoulder and when one looked round, there would be a long row of teeth snapping at us with its wooden jaws. It was frightening for a child. Usually, there would be a man leading the horse, with a rope, and another covered over with sacks or blankets as the horse.

Percy Maylam's account of the Deal Hooden Horse shows that the custom had declined to two performers by 1907. Two further accounts of the Hooden Horse at Deal at the turn of the century survive in the Deal Maritime Museum, one calling it the 'Green Horse' and mentioning that it was accompanied by handbell ringing, and the other from a member of a Deal boatman's family, who remembers it as the 'Ogling Horse':

> Then there was the Ogling Horse... the hooded horse of Queen Elizabeth's reign, a man under a sack, with a wooden head something like a horse with two large clappers for a mouth, the man clapped them together with a terrible noise but that was part of Christmas.

The Deal Hoodening tradition was distinctive in being run by fishermen as opposed to farmhands.

A number of traditional carved Hooden Horse heads survive. Maidstone Museum has two, found in a barn at Wingham, given to Wye College, who in turn donated them to the Museum, who unfortunately rarely display them. Deal Museum is very helpful about the two it has recently been given by Folkestone Library, one of which is that photographed by Percy Maylam at Walmer and the other a modern horse carved in the traditional style. The horse photographed by Maylam at St Nicholas-at-Wade, called Dobbin, is also thought to have survived and to be the one used by the revival team there; a second early horse, Black Beauty or Young Dobbin, was obtained from a Canterbury antique shop in 1976, who in turn bought it from a gallery in Flimwell, Sussex. The landlord of the Gate Inn, Marshside, owns the Chislet Horse, found hanging in a barn at Hoath in 1974 and thought to be made in the village in the late nineteenth century. Although the custom has no traditional connection with morris dancing, morris sides from the 1930s have helped to preserve the custom and several teams feature a Hooden Horse as their morris totem animal; the East Kent Morris Men have two horses made in Folkestone about 1953.

Percy Maylam's book and the surviving horses have been major factors in the formation of revival teams at St Nicholas-at-Wade (where they now write an annual village play to go with the custom), Whitstable (where the horse dates to about 1980, but with older trimmings) and Deal (a horse with green sacking made around 1995) and new sides including Wickhambreaux, Sandling and our own team – the Tonbridge Hoodeners, the most westerly of the teams, which features a death and resurrection play based on an amalgamation of horse plays from other parts of the country written by Geoff Doel and Nick Miller. Together with Percy Maylam's great nephew Richard and Mick Lynn, Geoff has resissued Percy's book with accompanying essays at an accessible price. He has also founded the Canterbury Hoodeners with James Frost, who mounted major exhibitions on the Hooden Horse in 2023 at Maidstone & Herne Bay Museums, with a fine associated scholarly book published by Ben Jones of the St Nicholas team.

Handbell Ringing

As we have seen, some hoodening accounts mention associated handbell ringing, but this is a distinct custom practised all year round in Kent and elsewhere, but handbell ringers were always particularly in demand at Christmas. Hop farmer and traditional singer Ken Thompson remembered his father ringing handbells on Christmas Eve 1923 at the family farm at Little Betsoms:

> ...I was wakened by the sound of ringing bells. I climbed out of my cot and opened the door into the living room where, to my amazement, I saw a number of whiskery men standing all round the room. The fire was flowing and it reflected their ruddy tanned faces and brass bells shining in their hands... I can see them now, their old faces shining. They'd obviously had a drink and were enjoying themselves. The oldest men seemed to have one bell in each hand, the others, two bells in each hand and then there was my

father. I can remember even now the pride with which in later days he used to say, "I had to play four in each hand." When they turned their wrists the Christmas tunes rang out.

Ken remembers his mother singing the gothic Christmas ballad 'The Mistletoe Bough' (written by Thomas Bayly in the early nineteenth century) and it was also in his repertoire and sung by him at the Tonbridge Folk Club. The song concerns a bride trapped in an old chest whilst playing hide and seek. Traditional singer Les Waghorn remembered hearing it sung between the wars in the Headcorn area:

> *The mistletoe hung from the Castle wall*
> *The holly bough hung in the old oak hall*
> *And the Baron's retainers were blithe and gay*
> *All keeping their Christmas holiday.*

Feasting

In the Middle Ages, royalty and the aristocracy celebrated the Twelve Days of Christmas in festive style. *The Croyland Chronicle* describes Edward IV's 1482 Christmas at Eltham Palace. The King was 'clad in a great variety of most costly garments, of quite different cut from those which had hitherto been seen in our country'. There were two thousand guests and the food supplied for the twelve days of Christmas were as follows:

> 1,000 sheep, 2,000 swans, 6 bulls, 400 peacocks, 4,000 bitterns, 4,000 dishes of jelly, 1,000 cold venison pastries, 300 calves, 1,000 geese, 1,200 plovers, 200 cranes, 200 heronshaws, 2,000 hot custards, 15,000 hot venison pastries, 800 pigs, 2,000 capons, 2,400 quails, 2,000 kids, 1,000 curlews, 12 porpoises and seals and plenty of spices, sugared delicacies and wafers.

An interesting custom last documented at Walmer was to give cocks extra food on Christmas Eve so that they would spot any evil spirits abroad. Their special cake, made of fat and grain, was called 'the Christmas Sheaf' and is apparently still fed to birds on the local duck pond on Christmas Eve.

Puritan Assault on Christmas

In the seventeenth century, Canterbury was a battleground for the very survival of the celebration of Christmas in the Civil War. Loyalties in

Canterbury were sharply divided between the Royalist and Parliamentarian causes and when the Puritan Mayor, William Bridge, proclaimed in December 1647 that by order of Parliament 'Christmas Days and all other superstitious festivals are utterly abolished', there was trouble! The Mayor proclaimed that the usual Saturday market would be held on Christmas Day and that all shops should open and that no church services were to be held. He threatened prosecution or arrest for anyone who hung 'rosemary, holly, or bayes or other superstitious herbs' at his door or made 'either plum pottage or nativity pies', hence the nickname of the ensuing disturbances – 'The Plum Pottage Riots'.

The Reverend Aldy of St Andrew's Church preached on Christmas Day in defiance of this proclamation, but the Puritans tried to disrupt the service by making noisy demonstrations outside the church. Twelve shops opened and the Royalists damaged their goods and tried to persuade them to close. Mayor Bridge toured Canterbury encouraging shopkeepers to open up and when receiving a rude answer from one, struck him in the face and then was himself seized upon and thrown into the gutter. This led to further assaults on Puritans; their windows were broken and their goods thrown about the streets. The Royalists barricaded St George's Gate, Burgate and Wincheap Gate with timber and their watchword was 'For God, King Charles and Kent'.

On Boxing Day, the mayor set a small armed guard under the leadership of Captain White, a barber, to watch the gate, and he shot one of the crowd for calling him a 'Roundhead', which caused a fresh riot. The citizens 'came forth with clubs' and assaulted and imprisoned Captain White and attacked the house of the mayor, who had fled. The citizens obtained the keys to the prison and set their own guards over the city. By 27 December the Royalist insurgents had increased to over 1,000; they took control of the Town Hall and with it a supply of arms and powder. When the sheriff intervened to try to rescue Captain White, 'he was knocked down and his head fearfully broke; it was God's mercy his brains were not beat out'. Other Puritans were attacked, including a Thomas Harris, who was described as 'a busy prating fellow'.

Eventually the Justices of the Peace persuaded the citizens to lay down their arms on condition that no retribution would be taken against them. However, the mayor brought in 3,000 Roundhead soldiers, who damaged the city gates and walls and imprisoned the Justices in Leeds Castle for two months. Some of the rioters were imprisoned and tried, including the poet Francis Lovelace, who wrote his famous poem *To Althea From Prison*, with its famous line 'Stone walls do not a prison make', during his incarceration.

The jury found the defendants not guilty and organised a petition requesting that king and Parliament should settle 'the Peace both of Church and Commonwealth'. The reaction of Parliament to this petition was to threaten to hang two petitioners from each parish which lead to a general Royalist uprising in Kent, defeated in a pitched battle at Maidstone. Not until the restoration of the 'Merry Monarch' Charles II in 1660 could Christmas be properly celebrated. Appropriately the king landed in Kent, greeted symbolically by the erection of two maypoles at Deal – maypoles had also been banned by the Puritan Parliament.

Christmas Superstitions

Sidney Bredgar in an article in *The Invicta Magazine* entitled 'Some Curious Old Customs in East Kent' mentions two traditions which show belief in the veneration of the birth of Jesus by the natural world:

> The belief still survives that, on Christmas Eve, exactly at the hour of midnight, a certain rose slowly opens and re-closes its petals to salute the birthday of our Lord; and some of the old country folk also believe that, at the same moment, and for the same purpose, all the sheep in the meadows turn and bow towards the East.

The second of these traditions seems to be a Kent tradition parallel to one in Dorset, referred to by Thomas Hardy in *Tess of the D'Urbervilles* and his beautiful poem 'The Oxen', of the farm beasts kneeling at midnight on Christmas Eve.

Christmas Music and Songs

West Galley choirs (or quires) with stringed instruments sometimes augmented with serpents, clarinets and oboes were popular in Kent in the eighteenth and early nineteenth centuries and featured locally written carols and tunes. Thomas Clark, the Canterbury shoemaker, after whom the revival West Gallery group 'The Thomas Clark Choir' is named, wrote a Christmas setting for the psalm 'While Shepherds Watched Their Flocks By Night' known as 'Cranbrook', which later provided the tune for the 'anthem' of Yorkshire – 'On Ilkley Moor Baht 'At'. Biddenden had a choir of singers accompanied by bass viol and clarinet until 1850 and William Tarbutt of Cranbrook remembered the choir going out on Christmas morning round the village singing 'While Shepherds Watched'. Frittenden had a celebrated village band that toured the village playing carols on Christmas Eve, featuring bass drum, flugel horn, two cornets, French horn, trombone, euphonium, tuba and side-drum.

In 1936, Tom Muggleton of Sundridge, a trained army musician, recalled his youthful experiences with his band touring the big houses north west of Sevenoaks:

> It was Boxing Day morning fifty years ago, when we set out with our band to tour Brasted and Sundridge. After calling at Brasted Place we made our way to Coombe Bank, then the residence of Count de Baillet. Unfortunately, the Countess had a strong aversion to drums, and, what proved more unfortunate, was the fact that the band did not know this.
>
> We were playing a little waltz, when the bass drummer, who should have been beating softly, suddenly began to bang his drum vigorously. I looked up at him, but before I had time to stop him, a tall lady swept past me and with a folded umbrella whacked that drummer such a resounding smack on the side of his head that his cap was sent flying into the middle of the ring of musicians. With 'Stop it, will you?' The lady turned and vanished through the front door. It was the Countess.
>
> ...However, the band received a subscription on leaving and went away thanking their lucky stars that events had not turned out worse.
>
> Fortunately, their reception at other ports of call was not quite so robust. Tramping their way into Chevening, they visited the residence of Earl Stanhope, where their efforts were rewarded with tankards of good old ale brewed at the home with tasty Devonshire cheese, and a good subscription. That gave us a better heart after our previous damper. At Ide Hill and Chipstead their receptions were equally as warm.
>
> ...From Ide Hill, the band journeyed down to Brasted Chart, finishing at Heverswood, the residence of Mrs Henderson. Here the butler handed them a subscription, but on inspecting the players in their green uniforms he said: 'Well, this is the most respectable little band I have ever seen. I am sure you must play nicely, but I am sorry to say I cannot hear you, as I am stone deaf!

Sevenoaks News 24 December 1936.
Interview with Tom Muggleton of Spring Cottage, Sundridge

There is a distinctive Kentish version of 'The Seven Joys of Mary' said in 1889 in the Kent Archaeological Society's *Notes And Queries* to be 'a favourite with the Gravesend juveniles just before and at Christmas, when it may be repeatedly heard in the town and suburbs'. 'The Seven Joys' was a very popular carol, which derives from the medieval adoration of the Virgin. The Kent version is unusual in having Jesus 'ride above the sun' in the first verse and wearing the crucifix instead of being on it in verse six.

The Seven Joys of Mary
(Gravesend version)

The First good joy that Mary had
It was the joy of one,
To see her own son Jesus,
To ride above the sun,

REFRAIN
To ride above the sun, good man,
And blessed may He be;
Both Father, Son, and Holy Ghost,
To all eternity.

The next good joy that Mary had,
It was the joy of two,
To see her own son Jesus,
To make the lame to go.

The next good joy that Mary had,
It was the joy of three.
When that her own son Jesus
Did make the blind to see.

The next good joy that Mary had,
It was the joy of four,
To see her own son Jesus,
To read the Scriptures o'er.

The next good joy that Mary had,
It was the joy of five,
To see her own son Jesus,
To raise the dead to life.

The next good joy that Mary had,
It was the joy of six,
To see her own son Jesus,
To wear the Crucifix.

The next good joy that May had
It was the joy of seven,
To see her own son Jesus,
To wear the crown of heaven.

The same *Notes and Queries* source also refers (in a letter dated 29 December 1888) to a Gravesend version of the carol 'I Saw Three Ships' entitled 'The Sunny Bank':

The Sunny Bank

As I sat on a sunny bank,
A sunny bank, a sunny bank,
As I sat on a sunny bank,
On Christmas day in the morning.

I spied three ships come sailing by,
Come sailing by, come sailing by,
I spied three ships come sailing by,
On Christmas day in the morning.

And who should be with these three ships,
With these three ships, with these three ships.
And who should be with these three ships,
But Joseph and his fair lady.

Then he did whistle, she did sing,
And all the bells on the earth did ring,
For joy that our Saviour was born,
On Christmas day in the morning.

New Year Gifts

The giving of gifts at Midwinter stems from both the Roman and pagan Anglo-Saxon cultures. Surviving records for England in general and Kent in particular for medieval, Elizabethan and Jacobean times mainly refer to the upper classes and show that gifts were more often given at New Year then Christmas. But Geoffrey Chaucer, a page in the household of Elizabeth, Countess of Ulster (wife of Prince Lionel) was given 20s 'for necessaries at Christmas' in December 1367. His wife Philippa, when in service with John of Gaunt, was given a New Year's gift of a silver-gilt buttoner with six buttons in 1373 and she received silver-gilt cups for New Year's gifts in 1380-82. Geoffrey was also working for Gaunt at this time, to be with his wife (Gaunt later married Philippa's sister) and a comic remark in *The Canterbury Tales* suggests that the Chaucers (or possibly just Geoffrey after his wife's death) lived at Greenwich for a period.

In the Tudor and Jacobean periods it was customary for the monarch to exchange New Year gifts with leading subjects. In 1532, Anne Boleyn, whose Kentish family seat was Hever Castle and whose mother and sister are believed to have preceded her as Henry VIII's mistresses, gave Henry an exotic set of richly decorated Pyrenean boar spears as a New Year's gift. Henry gave Anne a matching set of hangings for her room and bed in cloth-of-gold, cloth-of silver and richly embroidered crimson satin.

Sir Philip Sidney of Penshurst Place – celebrated poet, soldier and statesman – was at Court on New Year's Day 1578 and gave Queen Elizabeth 'a cambric chemise, wrought with black work, and a pair of ruffs set with spangles'. The Queen gave Sir Philip 'some gilt plate, weighing twenty-two ounces'. He later offended the Queen by opposing the suggested marriage alliance between Elizabeth and the Duc d'Anjou. Sir Philip's New Year gifts to the Queen in 1581 were thus highly symbolic – 'a whip to show that he had been scourged, a chain, to chain him to Her Majesty, and a heart of gold, to show that he was now entirely hers'. It is probably on this occasion that Queen Elizabeth reciprocated by giving Sir Philip the portrait of herself by Zucchero which still hangs at Penshurst Place.

Lady Anne Clifford was very friendly with Queen Anne, wife of James I, and her diary survives for part of the time she lived at Knole House in Knole Park near Sevenoaks. She records in her diary for December 1616, 'Upon the 31st I sent Thomas Woodgate with a sweet bag to the Queen for a New year's Gift, & a Standish to Mrs Hanns, both cost me about 16 or 17 pounds'. The diary records for 1619 that on 1 January 'I sent the Queen a New Year's Gift, a cloth of silver Cushion embroidered richly with the King of Denmark's Arms, and all one with stripes of Tent Stitch'.

The diaries do not record any reciprocal gifts sent by the Queen; the Queen was seriously ill in January 1619 and the diary records her death in March and Lady Anne's presence as a mourner at the funeral in May.

Blessing the Plough

Spring ploughing began in early January and although we have no early records for a 'Blessing the Plough' custom in Kent, Staplehurst Church started a modern tradition of plough blessing on Plough Sunday (the first Sunday after Twelfth Night) back in the 1950s, which is still going strong.

New Year Prognostications of the Future

Events happening at New Year or in January were thought to prognosticate on the pattern of events for the year as a whole. An example of this is a weather proverb relating to St Vincent's Day (22 January):

Remember on St Vincent's Day,
If the sun his beams display,
Be sure to mark the transient beam,
While through the casement sheds a gleam.
For tis a token right clear
Of prosperous weather all the year.

3

SMUGGLING & LORE OF THE SEA

There is a colossal amount of smuggling lore relating to the county of Kent, consisting of the interesting blend of fact and fiction, of history and romantic embellishment, which is the stuff of folklore. Traditional smuggling tales and memoirs of erstwhile smugglers can be checked against documents such as the two thousand surviving letters of John Collier, Surveyor-General of Riding Officers in Kent and Sussex from 1735-50, giving details about smuggling activities in those two counties.

The earliest smugglers were exporters (known along the south coast as 'owlers' owing to their night time activity) who smuggled raw wool across the Channel to avoid the severe restrictions protecting the English weaving industry. The Supervisor of Customs in Kent and Sussex complained in 1697 that most of the fleece shorn from the 160,000 sheep on Romney Marsh would be sent 'hot into France'. The Riding officers vigorously tackled export smuggling on the Marsh at the beginning of the eighteenth century and the coast between the Swale and the North Foreland, particularly Herne Bay, became the most lucrative export smuggling area in Kent. Export smuggling continued until the early nineteenth century, overlapping with the far more prolific import smuggling, which became significant in the eighteenth century, with the considerable import duties levied on luxury items such as brandy, rum, tobacco, tea, silks and muslins; so high were these duties, that smugglers could sell goods for as little as a quarter of their import price and still make a good profit. Kent fishermen were at the sharp end of smuggling luxury goods picked up from the French coast and for a time operated a two-way smuggling system, taking wool into France on the outward trip.

Whole communities within reach of the coast assisted with smuggling, often discreetly supported by gentry and clergy who benefited from the end results. The general outrage at the exorbitant duties, plus the fact that the smugglers had purchased rather than stolen the goods they were selling, and the undoubted necessary economic benefits to communities affected by low agricultural wages and rising food prices, caused many to view smuggling with an amused tolerance, as a way of outwitting harsh authority. A local factor in Kent was the ill will and economic losses caused in the eighteenth century through the Cinque Ports losing their privileges of importing goods without paying duty which they had held in recognition of their prominent role in supplying the crown with warships in time of war. By the mid-eighteenth century large numbers of men in Dover, for example, were totally reliant on smuggling for their livelihood. A customs entry of the same period records that 'most of the inhabitants of Folkestone, Sandgate and Hythe are in the confidence of the smugglers'.

The ruthless exploitation of the large Kent smuggling gangs, organised by shady financiers and protection racketeers (often from outside the locality) and increasingly violent, changed attitudes in some areas of Kent where the gangs were feared. The folklore of Kent smuggling reflects both the amused tolerance and the fear.

Spirits were usually smuggled in 'tubs' – half ankers holding just over four gallons. Tobacco, lace and silks, were stored in oilskin packages bound up with yarn supplied from large French warehouses at Dunkirk, Calais, Boulogne, Fécamp and Roscoff. By the late eighteenth century it was estimated that two thirds of the tea drunk in Britain was smuggled. Locally organised 'traditional' smugglers tried to avoid violence, but the large-scale gangs carried weapons and their smugglers were often escorted by armed guards as they carried the goods to staging posts at inland towns such as Hawkhurst, for transfer to London. The Smuggling Act of 1736 imposed the death penalty for wounding a Revenue officer and flogging, hard labour, transportation to America or serving in the Navy for unarmed resistance.

In the eighteenth century the revenue men were outnumbered and poorly paid, and the conscientious ones were in some danger. A customs officer watching a cricket match at inland Bromley in 1742 was attacked by smugglers with a vendetta against him; they stole his horse and he was forced to take refuge in Bromley College. The effectiveness against the odds, the bravery and the tenacity of many excisemen is exemplified by Richard Barham's legendary Exciseman Gill in *The Ingoldsby Legends*, who sells his soul to the Devil in order to procure a horse fast enough to catch Smuggler Bill! A real-life exciseman lay on top of the ruined walls of All Saints Church, Hope, near Dymchurch, in order to overhear smuggling plans; he subsequently seized the smuggled goods and arrested the smugglers.

Revenue cutters sometimes intercepted smuggled goods at sea. In 1771 a smugglers' ship bound for Dover was intercepted and in the ensuing struggle an exciseman was knocked overboard. Two ships then pursued the smugglers into Dover and tried to seize the goods on the beach, but were prevented by the locals who pelted the revenue officers with stones. Incited by the violence, one exciseman killed a smuggler and wounded another with his blunderbuss and the smugglers abandoned 150 tubs of brandy. Large Folkestone cutters smuggled tea from Flushing in the eighteenth century, being met by smaller vessels offshore from Folkestone. A Folkestone ship was captured in 1822 and its smugglers imprisoned in Dover gaol, from where they were rescued by colleagues and relatives.

Since smugglers had paid for their goods (albeit it at much reduced prices) they regarded them as their property and went to inordinate lengths to retrieve them. In 1780 the shipwreck of a smuggling boat near Whitstable led to the seizure of 183 tubs of Geneva, which was taken towards Canterbury under armed guard by nine dragoons. Fifty smugglers attacked them at Borstal Hill; two dragoons were killed and several wounded and the smugglers regained the tubs of spirits.

There were a number of infamous well-organised smuggling gangs operating in Kent. The North Kent Gang operated from the 1780s along a large swathe of estuary and coast from Chalk to Ramsgate. Reculver was one of their favourite landing places and they stored the goods at Margate Caves and Burntwick Island at the mouth of the Medway. The first account of the gang using violence is in 1820 – on two occasions – and it also released some of its members from Faversham gaol by force. In 1821 the gang murdered Midshipman Snow and five of their number were tried at the Old Bailey, but acquitted (juries were often sympathetic towards smugglers). After a further violent encounter in Marsh Nay, Westgate on Sea, eighteen smugglers were arrested, charged and found guilty; four were hanged on Penenden Heath, Maidstone, and the others transported for life to Tasmania.

The Hawkhurst Gang became notorious for violence and extortion as well as smuggling in the early eighteenth century under the leadership of

Arthur Gray who organised a large network of farm labourers as carriers from Poole in the west to Folkestone. The Gang's activities were very profitable and Gray built a mansion (later known as Gray's Folly) at Seacox Heath, near Hawkhurst. The Gang claimed to be able to raise a force of 500 mounted and armed men within an hour at their headquarters at the Oak and Ivy Inn, Hawkhurst. The Gang began as tea smugglers, but when the duty was cut in 1745 they turned to spirits and tobacco and also some highway robbery. Their next leader, Thomas Kingsmill increasingly moved away from traditional smuggling and smuggling ethics and the violence increased. The Gang brutally flogged Revenue officers and landed them in France (then at war with Britain) and terrorised villages, particularly Goudhurst, where they drank at the Star and Eagle Inn and used the house 'Spyways', overlooking the High Street. The Gang (fatally for them) began to neglect the time-honoured practice of rewarding those from whom they had borrowed horses, carts or equipment, or whom they had imposed upon for storage of goods and they increasingly turned to highway robbery, extortion and plundering houses, and to the murder or torture of those who resisted them or tried to bring them to justice.

Considerable written material, folklore and collected anecdotes from participants and, observers and their descendants survive about the famous 'Battle of Goudhurst'. Local historians have been able to piece together a detailed record of what happened, with considerable factual and topographical detail and re-enactments, festivals and local talks and research continue.

By 1747 the villagers were contemplating the desperate step of evacuating Goudhurst, but were saved by the resolution and military knowledge of a local soldier, George Sturt, who formed 'The Goudhurst Band of Militia' with the intention of resisting the demands and threats of the smugglers. The Hawkhurst Gang captured and tortured one of the militia and sent him to warn the villagers that they would be attacked at a specified time by a hundred smugglers who would kill, plunder and burn. Sturt ordered two hundredweight of gunpowder and arranged for the casting of musket balls, the erecting of barricades and the digging of trenches and strategically placed armed men on rooftop positions.

The smugglers attacked on 28 April 1747, stripped to the waist and armed with pistols, cutlasses and bats. The Hawkhurst Gang were routed; Kingsmill's brother and two other smugglers were killed and many others wounded and put on trial. Goudhurst was safe, but it took three other brutal murders before the authorities offered free pardons for evidence against the gang, which enabled them to prosecute and execute the leading active members. As usual the shadowy financiers escaped detection. A witness at one of the trials of Hawkhurst gang members described their methods:

> The captain of the cutter fixes a time and place where he designs to land, and seldom or never fails, being pretty punctual as to time, if the weather permits. As the master smugglers cannot fetch all the goods themselves, so they hire men whom they call 'riders', and they allow each man half a guinea a journey, and bear all the expenses of eating and drinking, and horse, and allowance of a dollop of tea, which is forty pounds weight, being half of a bag, the profit of which dollop, even the most ordinary sort, is worth more than a guinea, and some twenty five shillings, and some more: and they always make one journey, sometimes two and sometimes three in a week, which is indeed such a temptation that very few people in the country can withstand, and which has been the cause of so many turning.

A later gang, Aldington, operated on the edge of Romney Marsh in the 1820s, controlling coastal smuggling between Dover and Rye, with an inland transport route from Hythe to Ashford. The leader of the Aldington Gang was George Ransley, a farmer, who protected his smugglers with batmen armed with muskets and even provided a doctor to take care of wounded smugglers and paid sick benefit to their families, rather after the manner of the newly emerging Benefit Societies for farm labourers. The main headquarters of the Aldington Gang was the 'Walnut Tree' pub in the village and Ransley unofficially sold smuggled liquor from his cottage, which was locally known as 'The Bourne Tap'.

In 1821, the Aldington Gang were involved in 'The Battle of Brookland' in which five men died and over twenty were wounded. Two smugglers were put on trial for murder. Richard Wraight was acquitted after claiming that his involvement in the incident was accidental but Cephas Quested had mistaken a midshipman for a smuggler during the fight and handed him a musket, telling him to 'blow an officer's brains out' and been arrested by him. Quested refused to turn King's evidence against his colleagues and was hanged.

The Aldington Gang used Bilsington Priory (then a farmhouse) to store smuggled goods and spread ghostly stories about a disembodied and floating severed head to encourage the locals to keep their distance. As with the Hawkhurst Gang, the Aldington Gang lost local support through excessively bad behaviour, and for crimes which extended beyond the province of smuggling. The murder of the well-respected quartermaster Richard Morgan at Dover, while he was trying to apprehend some of the smugglers by boat, was the death knell of the Aldington Gang. A large reward to apprehend the murderers was offered and several informants came forward. Although Morgan had fired first, this was claimed to have been a warning shot. Nineteen smugglers were arrested and convicted, but the death sentences were commuted to transportation to Tasmania. George Ransley worked on a Tasmanian farm and, through good conduct, his wife and nine children were allowed to join him. He was eventually pardoned and rented his own farm in Tasmania.

Three well-known Kentish fiction writers drew on traditions of the Aldington Gang. Richard Barham, the vicar of Warehorne and Snargate and author of *The Ingoldsby Legends*, a mixture of folklore and fiction, knew the Gang and sometimes saw them at work on Romney Marsh, giving his name when challenged; he frequently noticed a strong tobacco smell in the tower of Snargate Church. His poem 'The Smuggler's Leap' may involve a tradition of the Aldington Gang, who used Reculver extensively for landings. Barham comments:

> Near this hamlet (Acol) is a long-disused chalk pit... known by the name of 'The Smuggler's Leap'. The tradition of the parish runs that a riding officer from Sandwich, called Anthony Gill, lost his life here... while in pursuit of a smuggler. A fog coming on, both parties went over the precipice... The spot has, of course, been haunted ever since.

G.P.R. James' novel *The Smuggler* is set around Hythe and features 'the Ramley Gang', clearly based on the Ransley Gang.

Russell Thorndike's fictional smuggling parson, Doctor Syn, is so well known that many people think he really existed. The Ship Inn at Dymchurch is frequently mentioned in the seven books about Doctor Syn and certainly was the haunt of smugglers and researched (along with other local sites and traditions) by Thorndike, who lived nearby; a secret hidey hole was discovered in the chimney breast of the pub, with smuggled spirits still inside. A celebratory 'Day of Syn' is held every second year in August at Dymchurch. The geographical, social and historical ethos of the Doctor Syn stories is so well researched that, though fictional, they provide a good example of Aristotle's theory of 'symbolic truth' and the Doctor Syn stories with their dark humour, cynicism and self-interest, yet combined at times with comitatus and some social solidarity are an unsentimental antidote to the more romantic picture of smuggling of the late Victorian age.

After the Napoleonic Wars more men and resources were devoted to blockading the Kent coast and to catching smugglers rather than just seizing smuggled goods. Smugglers were said to take pride in not abandoning wounded comrades. In 1827 a clash with the blockade men at Fairlight resulted in the deaths of three smugglers and the wounding of several more. Traditions relate that the wounded were carried to safety by their comrades, one smuggler carrying a comrade for six miles to Udimore. The traditions emphasise the *comitatus* of the smugglers and sometimes endow their deeds with heroism.

The abolition of many import duties in 1831 signalled the end of the traditional smuggling of luxury goods into Britain and the popularity of free trade in the high Victorian period confirmed its death, although Charles Dickens was still coming across evidence of smuggling in his Broadstairs summer residence, Bleak House, in the 1850s.

There are a large number of sites traditionally associated with smuggling in Kent. Faversham and Whitstable were noted for their oyster fishing and oyster boats carried contraband up Faversham Creek for the goods to be landed on the sheltered sandy beaches and sold at Faversham Market. Island Wall, a street running parallel to the raised protective shingle bank at Whitstable, was also the centre of a lucrative smuggling trade. Smuggled goods were also transported to Canterbury by packhorse and often taken on to London.

Margate, Broadstairs and Ramsgate originated as small fishing ports and had connections with the Cinque Ports and their traditions of free trade. Smugglers in that cliff top part of Kent carved out tunnels and used tracks carved out of the chalk cliffs by farmers who wished to use seaweed as fertiliser. Pegwell Bay, near Ramsgate, was a favourite landing place for Kent smugglers, with storage caves and tunnels to the cliff top and to the Belle Vue Tavern. Daniel Defoe, on a visit to Broadstairs in 1723, noted that few of the locals seemed to have regular jobs. Sandwich Bay was another regular landing place.

Deal was renowned for its small and medium-sized boatbuilding and in the eighteenth century the boatbuilders developed long, light, fast boats called galleys which were ideal for smuggling. They had small sails, space for twenty oarsmen, and could cross the English Channel in five hours in favourable conditions. William Pitt, the Prime Minister, ordered the destruction of boats on the foreshore of Deal in 1784, because of their involvement in smuggling. The Deal smugglers put to good use their knowledge of the Goodwin Sands to dodge the Revenue men; according to tradition, galleys were sometimes beached and carried over the Goodwins at low tide to elude pursuit.

In Hythe St Leonard's Church was used for storing contraband and the Bell Inn has a tunnel connecting to its cellar, through which tubs were floated from the Mill Stream. There is a grisly Romney Marsh tradition of an informant whose body was dismembered and whose ghost searches for the scattered parts. And in Lydd churchyard is an epitaph to the smuggler George Walker, killed by Lieutenant Peatt:

> Let it be known that I am clay
> A base man took my life away
> Yet freely do I him forgive
> And hope in heaven we both shall live.

Notorious Kent smugglers included Samuel Johnson (known as 'Slippery Sam') who was born the son of a smuggler in 1730. He purchased a farmhouse at Petham, near Canterbury, to receive smuggled goods and stored them in a network of tunnels which he also used to escape from the Revenue collectors; he also hid weighted kegs in a large pond. He overpowered his jailer and escaped from a small window in Maidstone Gaol by using axle grease. However, at the age of thirty, he was hanged after shooting an excise officer and his body suspended in chains from a gibbet for two days. Andreus Kostler of Ramsgate was fined £150 and had a part of his cargo confiscated after flasks of Hollands (gin) were found in his eel pits.

Richard Joy, the Broadstairs smuggler, weighed twenty-five stones and was pressed into the Navy after being caught on a smuggling run; he was allowed a double ration of naval rum after proving that he could do the work of two men. Joy returned to smuggling and was drowned aged sixty-seven on a smuggling run.

Joss Snelling was born at St Peters, Broadstairs, and he escaped from a famous smuggling skirmish known as the 'Battle of Botany Bay' in 1769, in which eight smugglers died and Joss shot a riding officer. In 1803 Snelling and Jeff Mutton were captured by Revenue men on Kingsgate Beach with sixty-one kegs of spirits. They pleaded not guilty, claiming they had come across the tubs by chance whilst walking on the beach; the judge fined them £100. Snelling was fined another £100 after an incident at St Mildred's Bay in 1831. He was presented to the future Queen Victoria (who took summer holidays at Ramsgate as a young girl) as 'the famous Broadstairs smuggler' and died peacefully at the age of ninety-six.

The Press-Gang

Less popular than the smugglers was the press-gang, active in time of war when its activities were sanctioned by Act of Parliament. Contrary to popular belief, the press-gang was after skilled seamen (untrained inexperienced men would be a liability in battle), as these extracts from the letter-book of an eighteenth-century Dover merchant make clear:

(i) 31 July 1738: Friday last came in three boats of press-gangs, one rowed on board Westfield (one of the Channel-service captains) and took two men... The boat with my two men rowed out of the harbour, but having got a constable, he brought the other two Lieutenants in my counting house. Mr Gay Matson, deputy mayor, and Hollingbury came and threatening to secure them, they sent to the other Lieutenant and the two men were released... On that noise all our men remained at Calais... we make shift with old men.

(ii) 7 June 1739: The pier is in great consternation, all the men of the fishing boats were pressed early this morning, and none left but the Master and boys... They all come in and cannot find men, and our vessels are in the same condition, so that there must be protection got for them so soon as any are granted, for the men are not willing to go without protection.

'Protection' refers to the legal protection for seamen against being pressed, which could, with some difficulty, be obtained in certain circumstances for some merchant crews.

The Goodwin Sands

Much of the best Kentish sea lore is connected with the Goodwin Sands, the 'ship-swallower', which lie four miles out to sea and parallel to the coast between Deal and Ramsgate, and are about ten miles long and two miles wide. One of Antonio's ships is reported wrecked there in Shakespeare's *The Merchant of Venice*:

Antonio hath a ship of rich lading wrack'd on the narrow seas; the Goodwins I think they call the place, a very dangerous flat, and fatal, where the carcasses of many a tall ship lie buried, as they say.

Act III, scene 1, lines 2-6

The Goodwins seem to be named after Godwin, Earl of Wessex and father to King Harold; certainly both the Earl and his son owned them in turn. There are various Kent traditions about this; during stormy weather when ships were in danger, the Deal fishermen used to say that 'Earl Godwin and his court were hungry', a supernatural Earl Godwin being believed to hold court under the Sands. A more detailed tradition is cited by Frank Mundell in his book *Stories of the Lifeboat* (1894):

It is said that the site of the Goodwin Sands was at one time occupied by a low fertile island, called Lomea, and here lived the famous Earl Godwin. After the Battle of Hastings, William the Conqueror took possession of these estates, and bestowed them upon the Abbey of St Augustine at Canterbury. The abbot... used the funds with which it should have been maintained in building a steeple at Tenterden... The wall, which defended the island from the sea, being thus allowed to fall into a state of decay, was unable to withstand the storm that, in 1099, burst over Northern Europe, and the waves rushed in and overwhelmed the island. This gave rise to the saying, "Tenterden steeple was the cause of the Goodwin Sands".

Parish and Shaw's *Dictionary of Kent Dialect* traces the proverb and its variants back as far as Leland's *Itinerary* and a sixteenth-century sermon by Bishop Latimer, citing an old man who remembered that 'before Tenterden steeple was in building there was no manner of talking of any flat or sands that stop't up the haven; and therefore, I think that Tenterden steeple is the cause of the decay and destroying of Sandwich haven'. Variants of the proverb include 'Of many people it hath been said/That Tenterden steeple Sandwich haven hath decayed', as quoted by Hazlitt and 'Tenterden steeple made the Goodwin Sands' and a proverb for someone doing a foolish thing is 'Let him set up shop on Goodwin Sands'.

Alan Major, in his revision of the *Dictionary*, suggests that 'There may be a grain of truth to the "legend" which began... at a time when the nuns of Minster, Isle of Sheppey, owned land and property at Tenterden'.

The Goodwins are famous for ghost ships; particularly the *Lady Lovibund* wrecked off Deal in 1748 due, it is said, to a love disputation. The ghost of this ship was spotted on the anniversary of the sinking on 13 February 1898 and 1948, but not unfortunately in 1998.

Fishing Lore

Dover was famous for soles and mackerel; in 'The Prologue to the Cook's Tale' in Chaucer's *The Canterbury Tales*, the Host asks the Cook to tell his tale:

> Now telle on, Roger, looke that it be good;
> For many a pastee hastow laten blood,
> And many a Jakke of Dovere hastow soold
> That hath been twies hoot and twies coold.
>
> lines 44345-8

A 'Jack of Dover' is a colloquial name for a Dover sole.

Dover mackerel fishers were called 'shotver men' and their nets' shot-nets; a local proverb says 'A north-east wind in May makes the Shotver-men a prey'. May was the start of the mackerel fishing season and a north-west wind was said to bring a good catch.

Pensioners at the Greenwich Naval Hospital were known as 'Greenwich Geese'. When a Gravesend fisherman married, he and his newly wedded wife were escorted by his colleagues to view his boat, festively decked out for the occasion.

Finally, we come to a sociable Christmas custom from Folkestone extant until around 1800 and recorded by *The Invicta Magazine*.

> The fishermen of Folkestone had a Christmas custom of their own. Eight of the largest and best whitings would be selected from the catch whenever a smack returned. These fish, known as 'rumball whitings', would be sold separately, and the money kept for providing a feast on Christmas Eve, which they called a RUMBALL. The skipper of each smack managed the feast for his crew and their friends, so there was the same number of feasts as there were boats. The custom seems to have fallen into desuetude about a century ago, but long afterwards Christmas Eve continued to be known as 'rumball night', and was set apart for social festivities. It has been suggested that the feast was originally instituted in honour of St Rumbald or Rumwold, whose protection of the fishery it was desired to obtain.

4

HOPPING DOWN IN KENT

The county of Kent was, for over 400 years, associated with the cultivation and harvesting of hops while the village of Little Chart claims to have Kent's oldest hop-garden, dating back to the introduction of the hop (*Humulus lupulus*) into England in the time of Elizabeth I. The harvesting of the hop was done by an itinerant workforce drawn from the gypsy population or London's East End, and many 'tinker' pickers came from as far away as Ireland. While working in the hop-gardens they were termed 'pickers' though many locals used the term 'furiners'. The picking 'season' in Kent started in early September and the harvesting could continue over a six-week period. Whole families were involved for women and children were allowed to pick on the fields, the little ones picking into umbrellas or boxes. Machine picking began to replace handpicking during the 1950s and eventually the 'furiners' workforce was no longer needed. Although lots of people are still alive from whom information can be collected, the rich folklore of the hop-picking tradition of the handpickers is now sadly a thing of the past.

In the nineteenth century, journalists observed and wrote magazine articles about Kentish hop-pickers and their customs for an interested middle class. The twentieth century saw transcribed from taped interviews lively accounts from the pickers about their experiences in the hop-fields and gardens, now considered important socio-historical records, and these, as well as hopping songs and poems, give us insight into how the harvesting of the hop generated its own customs, rituals and superstitions. Part of the charm and mystique of the Kentish hop yards was created by the special language indigenous to the work. Before the miniature hop was introduced, 'hopping stilts', ten to twelve feet high, were used by the men to do the 'stringing' and to unloose the bines: tools were used called 'hop dogs', 'hop peddlers' and 'hop spuds': the 'furiners' arrived in 'hopping specials' and were housed in 'hoppers huts'. In the early days the workers were familiar with 'tally sticks' and 'hop tokens' and ended their work with a 'hopping supper'. There were also ritual noises and cries associated with the hop-gardens – whistles or horns blown to signal to start or end the work or 'pull no more bines' shouted out in each of the gardens, indicating the last picking of the day.

The Pickers

In the nineteenth and early twentieth centuries, while hundreds of London's East-End pickers made their way to the Kentish hop-gardens in coster-barrows and pony carts, the poorest were prepared to walk twenty or thirty miles into the heart of Kent, often starting their journey along the Old Kent Road. From 1876 the South Eastern Railway provided 'Hoppers' Specials' which collected the pickers at Greenwich and New Cross Stations about three in the morning and ran through the night, usually employing old rolling stock, and, in the early days, cattle trucks. Oral accounts indicate that many children did not have tickets bought for them – it was more usual to secrete them under the women's long skirts or hide them in massive old prams that were heaped up with clothes, household items and tins of food being taken to the fields. For poor mothers this was an annual opportunity to earn enough money to buy the children winter boots or clothes while their menfolk in employment in London joined them at weekends. Those who have memories of hopping in its last phase in the 1950s and '60s confirm that the Londoners viewed the rail journey as a preface to an enjoyable six-week working holiday in the Kent countryside, for they 'sang all the way' often to concertina and accordion accompaniments. The Kent villagers were not so enamoured of the migrants and during the hopping season took elaborate precautions to protect their property, stock and shop supplies. In the early hours of the morning the trains were met with horses and carts (later, lorries) and the families conveyed to the various hop farms where they were allocated hoppers' tents or huts.

Accommodation for the Hoppers

This is a nineteenth-century account of the huts:

> The huts for the use of the hoppers stand in rows of eight houses; with a cook and wash-house in the middle; and are divided into eight compartments, each about twelve feet square. One company, numbering [up to] ten persons, is assigned to each compartment. The floor is thickly littered with straw for sleeping, but no chairs, forms or tables are provided. Hanging on an iron nail in the wall is an old lantern, in which the Hopper burns a candle. Washing conveniences are found by the Hoppers, and in many instances they bring bedding with them to lay over the straw... The cook and wash-house is usually in the centre of each row of huts. The front is open to the air; and there are three or four fireplaces in each. The farmer finds the Hoppers faggots for burning; affixes hooks on which to hang the kettles, and six pots can hang at one time over the fires. The huts are built with bricks, roofed with tiles and one storey in height... the washing... is done in the open air, and the hedges, or the grass, utilised for drying purposes.

Later huts were probably less substantial than earlier ones, with wooden walls and corrugated iron roofs. Although they still had outside fires, they were provided with chemical toilets and electric lighting, and tables were provided nearby on the 'common' – a field designated for the use of the pickers – so that the workers need not eat on the ground. Whole families were still accommodated within a tiny space 'but the pickers used to make them comfortable, and the fires got going outside of the huts at night. They used to paper them... and all the bugs in the world got behind them' (Ken Thompson, hop-farmer).

The following 'general regulations', drawn up to be exhibited in the nineteenth-century hop-gardens, give a good indication that smoking was always considered a fire risk by the farmer and that an excess of drinking often led to bad language and antisocial fracas amongst the hoppers.

GENERAL REGULATIONS

No lucifer matches to be used within the distance of five hills from a bin; no smoking allowed near the buildings or premises; no fire or light to be used after nine o'clock in the evening except on Saturdays, and no smoking allowed after that hour; no spirituous liquors to be sold or bought in the hop-gardens; no abusive, improper or immoral language to be made use of; and no quarrelling or fighting to take place. For any breach of these general orders, the person offending shall forfeit one shilling.

Some Kent publicans did not permit the hoppers to drink inside their pubs. After being served, the hoppers took their beer outside. There they congregated in groups, sometimes around a musician playing a concertina or melodeon, sometimes round a fire, and there would be some stepdancing in couples or singly and a lot of singing.

Faversham hop-farmer Ken Thompson's memories of the pickers in the late 1950s and early '60s were that men drove down in cars to see their womenfolk at the weekend and:

> [that on] Friday nights they'd all be up the pub singing 'Hopping Down in Kent'. They'd do a bit of dancing and the old mouth organs got going... They used to have a right old booze up. The pubs used to be full and some of the hoppers rolling about and the kids hanging about outside, some of them crying and some scrapping, and the others inside getting drunk and singing. They had a good time. They liked a drink.

In the nineteenth century the beer drinking hoppers among the workforce were often 'plagued' (their term) by middle class, well-meaning 'do-gooders' who were determined to stamp out excessive drunkenness amongst the lower orders.

The Advent of the Kent Missions

However, some 'do-gooders' were made very welcome and one – Father Richard Wilson, an Anglican priest with a parish in Stepney – became a legend. According to Miles Sargent, who in 1933 wrote an account of Wilson's time in the hop-fields, almost all of Wilson's congregation picked every September. So, in 1898, he decided to join them in the hop gardens and rented a cottage at Five Oaks Green – the first of three buildings which became better known as the 'Little Hoppers Hospital'. Here he worked with three nurses and all four gave their time and services free. Twenty-seven years later, in 1925, he started a new centre at Crowhurst staffed by Oxford undergraduates and medical students. Other missions followed, but the object of all was to give medical advice and to hold religious services on Sunday mornings and to provide a Sunday school for the children. Though the hoppers were generally immune to conversion, Father Wilson's young teams in the gardens were treated with affection and valued both for their medical help, and, pragmatically, for their tea-barrow which became a living tradition:

The "barrow" is a vehicle which holds a large tank which is filled with tea. It is then dragged or pushed up amongst the pickers who have been at work since seven-thirty, and large mugs of tea are sold at a halfpenny each. Cakes and buns are sold at the same time and provide a "levener" which is very welcome.

The water for the barrow is boiled up in a large boiler... known as "The Rocket". As we only burn wood, it needs a lot of attention... A tremendous amount of tradition has grown up around the travels of the barrow. It needs a team of at least four to work it properly, and the team has also to act as a male choir, since everything "down picking" is done with a song, and a dance too if possible. Its entry to the hop-lines is announced by the singing of two lines of a Yiddish song:

Yoi, yoi, what a gime it is
What a gime it is
Yoi, yoi!

This is sung to a very good plainsong melody, not of our invention; we took it over with the song. Then comes an hour or more of chaffering and back-chat. Jokes are cracked and personalities bandied to and fro, until the tanks run dry and the cakes are sold and the barrow bumps it way back to the Mission, to rest for another twenty-two hours. The surgery open at half-past nine for an hour, and special cases are then attended to.

From *St Francis of the Hop-Garden* by Miles Sargent

The missions disappeared with the last phase of hop-growing.

Tossing

People used to get tossed up in the hop pocket when people got excited.
Ken Thompson

Tossing young men and women in hop-pockets, particularly at the end of the harvesting, is one of the oldest recorded social customs in the Kentish hop-gardens. A hop-pocket consisted of a sturdy bin cloth attached to two solid wooden runners and was 6ft by 2ft. Few suffered any hurt as the 'pocket' was normally left half full of hops so that the fall was cushioned. George Orwell, who had himself gone hop-picking in the early 1930s as a prelude to using his experiences for *A Clergyman's Daughter*, observed the custom with interest and called it a 'queer' game and an 'old' custom.

Initiation into the Hop-Garden

Newcomers to the gardens were very often welcomed by having their shoes rubbed all over with hop leaves after which they were invited to offer a copper for 'shoe money'.

Child Control

Some children did get out of hand in the hop-fields and were punished by a slap from their parents with what was at hand – the thick and pliant stem of the hop – a painful punishment known as being 'given the bine'.

'Queen Hops', 'The Old Man', and The Hop Pillow

Finding a 'Queen hop' (a rather rare, extra-large hop) on the bine was equivalent to finding a four-leafed clover, and viewed by pickers as a luck-bringer. But the greatest of good luck was obtained from 'The Old Man', the last vine to be picked in each hop-garden. Another firmly held belief was in the efficacy of a hop-pillow (a small cushion stuffed with hop cones) which was claimed to induce sleep and was thought to help cure headaches and migraine.

Harvest Suppers

It became customary for many Kent farms to offer a harvest supper for the workers at the end of the picking. Sometimes it was set out in the oast house where the hops were dried. In the early days elected 'Kings and Queens of the Hop' were garlanded with hops and presided over the party. Other farmers chose to give a tea party for the children. At Beltring, Whitbread's Hop Farm, there was a Hop-Queen competition, entered by the prettiest girls from each of the hop-gardens. After her coronation, the elected 'Whitbread Queen' was dressed in a velvet cloak and given a bouquet of hops, after which she was drawn round the farm in a hop cart pulled by two shire horses. The last day of picking finished with a dance and, traditionally, a great deal of beer drinking.

'The Jovial Man of Kent'

This is the earliest known song about hops and is found in Chappell's *Old English Ditties*:

Away with all Wine-drinkers,
And such new-fangled thinkers,
And may they still be shrinkers
From all good men and true.
Thus said the Jovial Man of Kent,
As through his golden hops he went,
With sturdy limbs and brow unbent,
When Autumn's skies were blue above,
When Autumn's skies were blue.

The hop that swings so lightly,
The hop that glows so brightly,
Will sure be honoured rightly
By all good men and true.

Let the Frenchmen boast their straggling vine,
Which gives them draughts of meagre wine;
It cannot match this plant of mine,
When Autumn's... [refrain]

When winter snows are falling,
And winter winds are brawling,
For nut-brown ale are calling
All honest men and true.
And when the merry song is sung,
And logs upon the fire are flung,
They think upon the hop that swung,
When Autumn skies were blue above,
When Autumn skies were blue.

The Drowning at Hartlake Bridge

Many gipsies today make a point of visiting the bridge at Hartlake where they throw a wreath of hops into the Medway. These are the descendants of thirty gipsies who died in an accident here on 25 October 1853. Forty pickers – men, women and children – were being transported back on wagons to their hopping huts after a day's picking near the village of Hadlow. While crossing the bridge, one of the horses lost its footing and the cart crashed through the rotten wood fence sidings and tipped the occupants into the Medway. The river was in a high state of flood and thirty people were swept away and drowned. News of the deaths brought what seemed like 'all the [gipsy] tribes in England' to came to Hadlow. A pyramid-shaped memorial in the churchyard at Hadlow commem-orates their loss along with the names of the dead hop-pickers.

This simple and moving account comes in a letter from Alice Ransome written in 1984, describing the event as it was handed down orally in her family and is quoted verbatim here:

> What happened that black October night. My grannys grandmother and grandfather was hop picking nr. Paddock Wood. She said she had just put her to little boys to bed; one 4 one 3. The 4 year old become my grannys father when a young gipsy lad came on horse back to tell them what had happend. He was crying so much that they could nto make out what he was saying. At last he told them that thay was all drowned. He could not tell them no moor for he was in sutch a bad way. The old lady how lived in the cottage nr by told them to bring all the little gipsy children to the

cottage and she would look after them while the rest of the sipsies go and find out what was going on. Some of the man rod donkeys to the seen. The woman walked. When my grannys granny got ther she was met by her Aunt Emily, her mothers youngest sister. She cradle her niece in her arms and cried bitterly. She told her niece I have lost a dear sister and you have lost your dear mother. Thay say Toms little Tom was on her lap. Hes gone to. We can't find Thomas or Nat. We think they have been drowned (Thay was her to brothers) They was to powerful swimmers, thay was allways swimming. Thay was all up at the oast house when some one come and told them that their tents was all waterlogged, so that they had to go home and see what thay could save, but thay lost thier lives instead. It was terrible when thay draged ther lov ones out of the water. Grannys granny said she see her brother Thomas being draged out, she said the screams could be heard for miles. My grannys grandfther come and took hes wife from the seen beaucse she was with child. She was 4 months gon. The traveling people was coming from all over the place (for news travels fast amongst the Romany race) They comfort each other. Thay got all the little children together for ther was some little children how lost mothers fathers sisters and brothers. Relatives how come from afar trying to comfort the little ones. My grannys granny said ther was one little boy who never had no one. The only one he had was hes mother and she was drowed so he was left in the world all alone. Hes mothers boddy was hooked up by some old tree stumps and he was on top of her but he never new hes mother was under him untill he was pulled out. She saved his life. He sat on her coffin all the way to the burial. The gipsy said the farmer took the little boy. I dont no if that was right and some said the gipsies took him... The people of Hadlow and the nr. by villages was wonderful to them and my grannys granny never for got them. The gipsies would come back evry year to the memorial services My grannys grandparents come back every year no matter where thay was and she would throw a wreath of hops into the river and so would the rest of them who lost relatives on that Black October night.

A Postscript

Today the hop-fields have all but disappeared in Kent and the few hop-farms are no longer harvested manually. The beautiful and distinctive oast houses in which the Kent hops were once dried remain; however, most have been transformed into private houses.

5

THINGS HOLY
HEALING SAINTS, HOLY WELLS & HERMITS

The meeting of the powerful pagan king, Ethelbert (who believed himself to be descended from the god Woden), and forty monks from Rome on the isle of Thanet on the southeast coastline of Kent marks the beginning of the conversion of Anglo-Saxon Kent to Christianity and was described in an eighth-century work, Bede's *History of the English Church and People*:

> ...the king came to the island... and summoned Augustine and his companions to be brought to his presence while he was sitting in the open air... in case they were magicians... But the monks were filled with power from God... and approached the king bearing a silver cross as their standard.

Ethelbert, married to a Christian princess and alert to the possible political advantages of a link with Rome, was prepared to receive them kindly. The monks were allowed to go in procession to the royal capital, Canterbury, where they were given a house and permission to worship in the old Roman church of St Martin's (used by Queen Bertha) outside the walls. The work of conversion was rapid, for by 601, the year they arrived, the king had accepted Christianity and 10,000 of his Kentish subjects had either loyally submitted themselves for baptism or were summarily ordered to present themselves for conversion.

Saints

In the medieval Catholic past, a multiplicity of saints played a continuous and vital role in Kentish community life with the most ordinary Kentish person relating to and identifying closely with their regional as well as calendar saints, while the Virgin Mary received a special veneration both as saint and *Mater Genetrix* (the Mother of God).

Saints were vitally important in the Middle Ages: they were considered to be reflections of the godhead, a source of grace and a protective and benign presence that would pray for each individual at their hour of death. The physical building of any church, whether in village, hamlet or town, was considered to be the house of God, and was central to community life. Here the saints were 'housed'; all churches displayed images of saints, either in mural paintings, wood or alabaster. Here, also, birth, marriage and death was ritually celebrated by the community, here all sections of society met, the 'house' being left open to encourage day-time prayer, and where parishioners congregated to celebrate the various saints' days liturgically celebrated by the Church. Even the smallest church could be lavishly and colourfully decorated with paintings, murals, stained glass, decorated floor tiles, rood screens and, in the late Middle Ages, seating for the congregation with carved bench ends. The interior of each church was sanctified with holy water and made sweet with the smell of flowers, incense and wax candles, for fragrant smells were identified with sanctity. The linking of the community to the church became even more marked after 1215 when auricular confession and the taking of the sacrament became a yearly obligation for each and every member of the community.

Saints' lives became particularly well known in the late thirteenth century when many priests, preaching to a largely illiterate audience, used as sermon material a widely known text, the *Legenda aurea* (the Golden Legend), a collection of highly entertaining and morally uplifting (if sometimes historically dubious) stories, which were later published and thus available to an even wider audience. On the numerous Feast Days and Saints' days which marked their public holidays, Kentish societies and trade fraternities marched behind banners emblazoned with their particular saint's image, while saints images were taken from the church and paraded around the community before being returned to their pedestal, niche or altar. These were often occasions for a pageant, fair or feast. It could be said that the saints were as well known as television stars today; they had a reality, they were as approachable as old friends, they were amazingly helpful and versatile as well as being powerful; not only could they petition God on one's behalf, their relics were believed to have the potential to heal as could the holy 'oil' that was supposed to ooze from their reliquaries.

Kent's 'Work' Saints

Many of the best-loved saints during the Middle Ages in Kent were perceived as work-related 'patrons' and every industry and craft guild in Kent (as elsewhere in Britain) had its patron saint. The most important Kentish industries included fishing and farming, cloth-making and iron-working but tilers, brickmakers glassmakers, tanners, shoemakers, workers in wood, millers and bakers and merchants also had their 'work saints'.

Shoemakers, cobblers, tanners and leatherworkers had as their patron saints Crispin and Crispinian, early converts to Christianity who fled from religious persecution in Europe and were eventually put to death by the Emperor Maximilian (286-305). Though there is no foundation for the legend, it is claimed they settled at Faversham where 'they worked as shoemakers at a house in Preston Street, near the Crosse well, now the sign of the Swan [inn]... long a place of pilgrimage for other workers in the craft of which St Crispian is the special patron'. Henry V's speech exhorting the English before the battle of Agincourt was made on 25 October, the eve of the saints' feast day:

> This day is call'd the feast of Crispian;
> He that outlives this day and comes safe home,
> Will... rouse him at the name of Crispian

Success in the battle was attributed to that saint as well as the patron saint of the English, St George.

Camden mentions a 'heap of larger stones' (thought to be near Greatstone, Dungeness) 'which locals claim to be the tomb of the saints Crispin and Crispinian, who they pretend were shipwreckt here'.

Early furnace sites have been identified in the Weald indicating important iron works in Kent. Every community likewise had its blacksmith; in the Middle Ages those who worked at these crafts would belong to an important guild (to which many women also belonged). The tenth-century saint who presided over these activities was St Dunstan (924-988). As a young hermit at Glastonbury, he had become expert in the crafts of the jeweller and the smith and continued to practise these skills during his twenty-eight years as Archbishop of Canterbury. He was considered a saint in his lifetime. The legend of his encounter with the Devil while working at his anvil in Mayfield (he tweaked the Devil's nose with his red hot tongs in order to expel him from his workshop) was one of the best-loved and best-known apocryphal medieval saint's legends. Kent tradition has it that the Devil bathed his throbbing nose in the 'wells at Tunbridge' thus producing curative spa waters. Another of his legends is associated with Canterbury.

One night, Dunstan dreamed that he was in heaven, attending a royal wedding feast. An angel harpist invited him to join in the marriage hymn but Dunstan demurred, for he had never heard either the words or the tune before. The harpist then played and sang both parts of an exquisite antiphon beginning '*O rex gentium dominator omnium*'. Dunstan listened intently and on awakening from his dream taught the Canterbury choristers both words and music. Ultimately Dunstan was elected patron saint of locksmiths, goldsmiths, silversmiths, jewellers, blacksmiths – and musicians. His cult in Kent was a very active one.

The Farmers' Saints

St Edith's birth may have initially caused scandal for she was the illegitimate daughter of King Edgar of England and a young noblewoman, Wulfryth, who, when she fell pregnant, was a novice-nun in the convent in Wilton. Wulfryth was sent far away to the village of Kemsing in Kent for the confinement. Like many illegitimate offspring and discarded royal mistresses of the period, both Edith and her mother ended their lives as nuns in an enclosed religious order, for her mother returned to the community at Wilton and was later elected Abbess. Edith chose to remain with her mother in the convent rather than live a life in the royal court and gained a reputation for holiness before she died, a nun, at the age of twenty-three. Miracles were quickly claimed at her tomb and a cult was established. In the Middle Ages, statues of St Edith were set up over the waters of the wells in Kemsing village and in the church. Lambarde, who visited the wells during the age of Elizabeth I, gives an account of the superstitious beliefs and practices of the day which indicate that the local farmers considered Edith the protector of their crops:

> Some seelie bodie, brought a pecke or two, or a bushell of corne, to the church, after praiers made, offered it to the image of the saint. Of this offering the priest used to toll the greatest portion, and then to take one handfull or little more of the residue (for you must consider he woulde bee sure to gaine by the bargaine), the which, after aspersion of holy water and mumbling of a fewe wordes of conjuration, he first dedicated it to the image of Saint Edith, and then delivered it backe to the partie that brought it, who departed with full persuasion that if he mingled that hallowed handfull with his seede corne it would preserve from harme and prosper in growthe the whole heape that she should sowe, were it never so great a stacke.

The Saints of the Sea

In the Middle Ages all journeys by water whether for pilgrimage, trading or fishing could be potentially dangerous. The Kent coast is full of busy ports and embarkation points to the continent but some parts of the east and south coasts of Kent are windswept and rocky, a potential hazard to sea traffic. St Nicholas, a fifth-century bishop of Myra, was perceived as the patron saint of sailors and some churches on the Kent coastline are dedicated to this saint. St Nicholas also impartially protected the smugglers who were operating from the coast – in the Middle Ages thieves were sometimes referred to as 'St Nicholas' Clerks' and the word 'nicking' is said to derive from this.

The Virgin Mary was seen as a super-saint, and could take any protective role for any group. Like Nicholas, she related to sea-going activities and one of her titles was 'Star of the Sea'. In Kent, the church of the Virgin of Broadstairs was the most famous of her sea-going chapels. Sailors, fishermen, and pilgrim vessels 'lowered the topsails of their ships by way of salute' when they saw the spire or its 'light'. There are numerous records of monetary gifts made to this chapel, as when one Richard Algode in the year 1479 'gave 4d to the Light of Blessed Mary of Brodestyr' either to ensure a safe sea journey or in gratitude for a successfully accomplished pilgrimage. The reference to the 'light' may be to a blue glass lantern which stood high on the cliff top so that 'Shyppes that lyith in ye narrow see with marchandyse for Tenet (Thanet) seith at the hedde of the Cliffe ye Shrine of the Bluw Light from many myle off'. Within the chapel a carved image of the Virgin faced out to sea, set on a high pillar.

Another of the Virgin's 'sea' chapels in Kent was 'Our Lady of the Rock', near Dover. Here, having survived a particularly stormy sea journey in 1532, Henry VIII offered 6s 8d in grateful thanks. Ironically, the chapel was very soon after destroyed by a violent storm.

Shipwrecks due to violent coastal storms inevitably became part of Kentish folklore. One Kent legend has it that the two medieval towers erected on the ancient church at Reculver were paid for by an abbess from a convent at Faversham who was shipwrecked while en route for the shrine of the Virgin of Broadstairs. The first tower was erected in memory of her dead sister (also a nun) who had perished in the same shipwreck, the second to act as a beacon to mariners. Edward Hasted in his *History of Kent* (vol. iii., p. 635) tells us that shipwrecks were such a regular occurrences at Reculver that Thomas Hammond, hermit of the chapel of St James in Reculver, during the reign of Richard III, was given special responsibility for 'the burial of persons who by storm or otherwise perished'. Drowning at sea was not the only hazard for travellers in Kent in the Middle Ages. Rickety bridges and deep or fast flowing rivers also presented problems. A tiny stone bridge chapel stood on the 'narrow and dangerous' wooden bridge at the Strood end of the River Medway and linked Strood with the Cathedral town of Rochester. It was built and dedicated to the Virgin in the early thirteenth century by Gilbert de Glanville, Bishop of Rochester (1185-1214). A delightful medieval 'Virgin Miracle' tale in verse tells the story of a troubadour, 'Harpur a Roucestre' who was blown off Rochester bridge in a gale and swept along the raging river Medway, calling on the Virgin for help, but never ceasing to play his harp. The Virgin hears his plea and he survives to tell his tale.

The Healing Saints

When people were sick in medieval times, only the rich could afford to seek the services of a doctor whose services were expensive, otherwise every housewife had her own herbal remedies. In addition, most sick people (rich and poor alike) applied to the saints for cures and often went on pilgrimage to 'healing shrines' or sent surrogate pilgrims there on their behalf. Reginald Scot who lived in Elizabethan times, compiled a list of healing saints from a medieval Latin manuscript recorded that:

> St John and S. Valentine excelled at the falling evil [scrofula]. St. Roch was good at the plague. S. Petronill at the ague ... For mad men and such as are possessed with divels, S. Romane was excellent and Friar Ruffine was also prettilie skilfull in that art. For botches and biles, Cosmos and Damina; S. Clare for the eies. S. Appolline for teeth, St. Job for the pox. And for sore brests, S. Agatha.

During the Middle Ages, Kent was fortunate to have the richest and most popular healing shrine in Britain, which attracted massive revenue to the county and gave it an international reputation – that of St Thomas à Becket (d. 1170), the martyred Archbishop of Canterbury. Chaucer's *Canterbury Tales*, written in the 1380s, are about a group of people heading for the shrine. Becket was claimed to cure every kind of disease and his shrine was run as a tremendously successful business by the monks of Canterbury Cathedral for many years until in 1538 Henry VIII had the gold- and gem-encrusted shrine dismantled, confiscated the wealth of the cathedral and destroyed all the relics. The story of Becket's bloody end in his own sanctuary Cathedral in 1170 at the hands of four of Henry II's liegemen, Reginald Fitzurse, William de Tracy, Richard le Breton and Hugh de Moreville, is scarcely less riveting than the record of Henry II's subsequent enforced humiliation at the hands of the Church when barefooted and bareheaded and in his shift he walked to Canterbury Cathedral before the stunned townspeople after which he endured a whipping at the hands of Bishop and Abbot and eighty of Becket's monk community before Becket's mutilated body (at that date enshrined in the crypt).

The beautiful thirteenth-century 'miracle' windows in the apse of Becket's Cathedral at Canterbury are a visual record of just some of the *miracula* (miracles) claimed for Becket by the monks who tended Becket's glittering shrine. There is William, a London priest – the first sick pilgrim to be cured by drinking 'the martyr's blood'. He is pictured standing beside Becket's first tomb holding a cup which contains holy water and into which a Canterbury monk spoons one drop of the martyr's healing blood. The windows also show the 'possessed' (mentally sick and insane) being taken before Thomas' shrine in hopes of being restored to mental health. In medieval as in biblical times, people suffering from epilepsy, dementia, schizophrenia, suicidal clinical depression, etc. were considered to be possessed by devils. The windows also indicate that through Thomas' intervention the blind were made to see, cripples given the use of their limbs, the drowned brought back to life, and lepers and plague victims restored to health. Becket's ability to cure diseases was very comprehensive. Royal visitors helped popularise the shrine and attracted wealth and fame to the county. Richard I, the Lionheart, walked in pilgrimage from Sandwich to Becket's shrine in Canterbury and attributed his successful siege of Acre to 'God and St Thomas'. King Louis VII of France believed that St Thomas had cured his sick son and accordingly gifted a magnificent ruby (the 'Regale') to the tomb in 1179. It may come as a surprise that Henry VIII had a particular devotion to St Thomas as a young man and visited the shrine several times. Every fiftieth anniversary of Becket's translation, 'indulgences' were granted to pilgrims, and attracted thousands of English and foreign pilgrims.

Just a mile from the Cathedral at Harbledown (Chaucer calls it 'Bob up and Down') was a leper colony, later to become almshouses for the poor, founded in 1084 by Archbishop Lanfranc. It was sited on the edge of the city outside the city walls and had its own church and priest and a community who were required to wear distinctive cloaks and veils and to carry rattles in addition to their begging boxes when they went abroad. The community boasted that they held a special relic – one of the shoes worn by Becket when he was martyred. Pilgrims visiting their church could be sprinkled with holy water from this shoe or kiss the buckle and it was considered to bring good luck and offer blessing and protection. Desiderius Erasmus, the humanist scholar, left a caustic account of his visit in which he refused to kiss the relic but nevertheless offered a monetary contribution.

Canterbury was not the only great Kentish cathedral to claim curative fame and to attract thousands of pilgrims. Rochester Cathedral held the relics of the pious Scottish baker, William of Perth, who had dedicated his entire life to good works and who was mugged and murdered by his adopted son, David, in the parish of St Margaret's near Maidstone while undertaking a pilgrimage to the Holy Land in 1201. William was later enshrined in Rochester Cathedral after a miraculous healing cure was claimed for him. One legend printed in *the Nova Legenda* in 1516, recounts that William's dead body was discovered in a remote place by a madwoman who wove a circlet of honeysuckle for his bloodstained head before leaving the corpse. Some days later she returned to the scene of the murder and placed the circlet on her own head whereupon she was restored to sanity. Her cure having been reported at Rochester, the townspeople brought William's body to the Cathedral, where he was interred. A chantry chapel was later built on the spot of the martyrdom and a shrine to the saint erected in the Cathedral where cures were reported. William was canonised in 1256.

Healing statues

Shrines alone were not unique in offering the possibility of healing cures for the sick in Kent. A much-frequented healing statue in the sixteenth century was that of the Virgin in the chapel of Our Lady of Court-at-Strete, near Canterbury. Here, Elizabeth Barton, the Holy Maid of Kent, put on a spectacular show in 1525. Lambarde reports that 'she entered the Chappell to the sounds of the choir singing *Ave Regina Caelorum* [Hail, Queen of Heaven]' and a company composed of Church commissioners, courtiers, and three thousand people besides 'the common sort of people in the Countrie'. Once before the statue, the young nun fell, as expected, into a fit, during which she amazingly recited the Virgin's praises in 'metricall and ryming speeches'. Tyndale in his *Answer to Sir Thomas More's Dialogue* witnessed her 'fit' and describes the 'stopping of her breath... grievous pangs... tormenting, disfiguring, drawing of her mouth awry, and... fearful, terrible countenance' which amazed all present. Because the Holy Maid was pronounced 'cured', the statue of Our Lady of Court-at-Strete not surprisingly gained a local reputation for performing healing miracles. Lambarde records that it permitted nursing mothers to lactate, 'moistning womens breastes that before were drie and wanted milke', as well as 'restoring all sorts of sicke to perfect health, reducing the dead to life againe, and finally dooing al good, to all such as were measured and vowed (as the popish maner was) unto her at Court of Strete'. To be 'measured and vowed' in 'the popish maner' was to have a wick cut the length of one's height. This was inserted into wax and burnt as a votive candle before the saint's image.

Yet another Kent statue accredited with amazing properties was that of the Apostle St Bartholomew (known as 'Bartilmew') of Otford who was applied to locally to make barren women fertile. Lambarde tells us that women desperately anxious to have a son, prayed to and left a candle votive offering before the statue. An additional part of the ritual was to give the parish priest, in the name of St Bartholomew, 'a cocke chicken'. If a baby girl was wanted, the priest was accordingly presented with a hen.

Another cult of interest was that of 'Master' or 'Sir' John Shorne of Buckinghamshire (the latter a courtesy title for priests). Prayers before statues of this holy man were reputed to cure the ague (fever) and gout as did water from the numerous wells he is said to have blessed. Shorne lived in the late thirteenth century and, though venerated in a number of counties including Kent, was never canonised. An erstwhile monk of the Augustinian Priory at Dunstable, he later became priest at North Marston in Buckinghamshire and quickly gained a reputation locally for his piety. It was claimed that he spent so much time on his knees praying that the skin on his knees had turned to horn. There was an altar with his image in Canterbury Cathedral, according to a sixteenth century account, and pilrims' badges were sold representing him preaching in a pulpit and holding a boot. The last is an illustration of an apocryphal story connected with him. It tells how he conjured the Devil into a boot after being severely tempted by the fiend. After this, the holy man blessed the boot and dispelled the evil it had contained.

Healing and Holy Wells

There are a numbers of springs and wells in Kent that have saintly dedications and a reputation for therapeutic powers. The giving of *ex voto* offerings to wells and springs in the belief that they may contain or be presided over by a supernatural power with the ability to heal is believed to date from a period of great antiquity. With the advent of Christianity, sacred healing wells and springs are believed to have often been rededicated to Christian saints.

In Canterbury crypt until the Reformation, there was a holy water well near the eastern end of a chapel dedicated to the Virgin Mary. Water from this was mixed with the 'martyr's blood' (that of Thomas à Becket) and sold as healing medicine in small lead phials called ampullae which could be carried away or worn round the neck.

There was another holy well associated with Becket at Otford mentioned by Lambarde. The well here was not claimed to have curative properties, but was thought to be miraculously created near to the Archbishop's palace and chapel. This is Lambarde's description:

> When St Thomas 'sawe that it [his palace] wanted [lacked] a fit spring to water it, he strake his staffe into the drie ground, in a place therof now called Sainct Thomas Well, and... immediately the same water appeared, which running plentiflly, serveth the offices of the new house, till this present day'.

There were several other Kentish 'Becket' wells claimed to effect cures during the Middle Ages. One was in Shorne Wood, another at Bapchild (originally sited near to a leper hospital), and one near Wateringbury, the latter locally visited by newlyweds in the hope that their offspring would be healthy. There is a tradition that Becket preached under an ancient yew tree, still standing in the churchyard at Capel.

The Black Prince's Well is still visible on the hillside near Harbledown road close to what was once the St Nicholas leper colony outside Canterbury. In the medieval period the well had a reputation for curing every kind of eye complaint (bleritis, conjunctivitis, glaucoma, eye injuries, etc) as well as leprosy. The medieval idea of leprosy was much more extensive than is ours today and included every kind of skin disease as well as sexually transmitted diseases. The Black Prince is said to have drunk from the well and to have asked for its waters on his deathbed in 1376. To commemorate this royal interest, the stone well head was later decorated with the Prince's insignia of the three feathers (a badge taken from the King of Bohemia at the Battle of Crécy).

St Blaise was a saint regularly applied to in the Middle Ages to cure every kind of sore throat, from tonsillitis to throat cancer. 'In the Bishop's Park at Bromley was a well and chapel dedicated to this saint, much frequented by the devout and where votive offerings were made'. (C. Seymour, *Survey of Kent*, 1776). Seymour claims that throughout the medieval period, an indulgence of forty days was granted to all those who visited the St Blaise chapel and well and offered their prayers there at Whitsuntide. The saint was particularly important in the Middle Ages as he was patron saint of wool-combers.

Another Kentish well which regularly attracted medieval pilgrims seeking cures, this time for eye-complaints, was that of St Eustace's healing well in the hamlet of Withersdane, near Wye. The claim that the saint had once visited Kent and blessed the holy well is described by one scholar as 'historically worthless' but remained popular in Kent.

Holy Curses

Kent has a lively tradition of cursing priests. Jerrold, citing Lambarde, quotes the well-known Kentish legend of St Thomas à Becket's curse on the men of Strood 'when being King's men, they cut the tail off the archbishop's horse.' The result of Becket's curse was that 'every one which came of that kindred of men which plaied that naughty prank, were born with tails, even as bruite beasts be'.

Christina Hole cites the legend printed by William Caxton that St Augustine cursed the snakes in the Isle of Thanet and drove them out:

> Thanatos, that is Tenet, is a ylonde besydes Kent and hath the name Thanatos, of deth of serpentes, for ther ben none. And the earth thereof sleeth serpentes yborn in other londes... Hit is supposed that this Llonde was halowed and blessed by St. Austyn, the first Doctour of Englishmen. Ffor ther he arrived first'.

Pre-Norman Female Saints in Kent and their Miracles

The miracle-working relics of St Eanswyth (d. 640), claimed by some to be the daughter of Eadbald, King of Kent, are recorded in the *Nova Legenda Angliae* and are quoted by Lambarde. Eanswyth was interred initially in her nunnery at Folkstone where she had died at the age of twenty-six. This convent may have been the first female monastic institution in England. There, according to legend, her relics:

> caused many wonders... she lengthened the beamme of a building three foote, [which]... the Carpenters had made... much too shorte... she haled and drewe water over the hills and rockes against nature from Swecton, a mile off, to her Oratorie at the Sea side... she forbad certaine ravenous birdes the countrey, which before did much harme thereabouts... she restored the blinde, cast out the Divell, and healed innumerable folkes of their infirmities.

After this catalogue of marvels, it is small wonder that after her death she was 'honoured for a Saint' and her shrine much visited. In 1885 a Saxon lead reliquary, which some believed to be that of the saint, was discovered, hidden within a cavity over the Easter Sepulchre in the parish church of St Mary and St Eanswyth in Folkestone. The saint features on one of the ancient Folkestone seals, holding two fishes in one hand and a pastoral staff in the other.

Saint Mildred was yet another royal nun with a strong local following in Kent. Having taken the veil in France, Mildred settled in Thanet with her community of nuns around 733. Legend has it that she was an excellent organiser and businesswoman, arranging for the grain on her highly productive convent farms to be shipped upriver to London where it was sold in Cheapside. One biographer tells us that she was roasted in a hot oven 'for three hours together' without being burnt which suggests some early medieval confusion over her relationship to the loaves of bread that were being baked from her corn. Many years later, when her convent was destroyed in a Danish attack, the Abbot of St Augustine's received permission from King Cnut to remove her sacred miracle-working relics to safety at Canterbury. Mildred's body reputedly had previously refused to be budged, but now she docilely permitted her remains to be transferred by the Canterbury monks, an obvious sign of her approval.

An even earlier Kentish legend is that of Mildred's mother, the Princess Domneva (also known by her Anglo-Saxon name, Ermenburga). Her two young brothers had been murdered by Egbert who saw them as rivals to the Kentish crown. A late and unhistorical account says that their bodies were buried under the floor of the king's throne room in the royal palace at Eastry and that God caused the bones to glow, thus revealing their presence and Edgar's complicity in the affair. The Archbishop of Canterbury, who was Egbert's confessor, advised him to offer the Princess Domneva *wergild* (compensation) for the boys' deaths. Domneva accepted a parcel of land in Thanet on which she founded a nunnery at Minster and where, as a widow, she became the first Abbess in around 670. More fanciful hagiographies say that she asked for a piece of land the size of which would be determined by the path taken by a hind running over the Kent countryside. The deer was released near Westgate, and followed to determine its path. As it crossed into Thanet it was attacked by three of the king's servants, Thunor, Dathan and Abiron, her brothers' assassins. The hind was miraculously saved from their spears when God caused the ground before their feet to open up and the evil men were 'hosed' into hell.

Lambarde uncharitably concludes that the Princess Eanwsyth of Folkestone, 'Queen Sexburge of Minster in the Isle of Sheppey and Princess Mildred in Tanet [Thanet]' were only honoured with sainthood because: 'first... They assured many great personnages unto them: secondly, they drewe (by the awe of their example) infinite numbers of the common people after them: And lastly, they adventured the more boldly (under those honourable, and glorious names and titles) to publish their peevish and pelting miracles'. New scholarship suggests that though their miracles may be spurious, and the more bizarre elements in their legends discounted, there is little to prove that these nuns and abbesses did not lead good Christian lives. Additionally, there is no doubt that their orders provided a safe refuge for a number of widows and other females who 'lodged' with the communities, and also that they provided charity and support for the poor locally.

The Flowering Stick

The *Anglo-Saxon Chronicle* gives a sober account of the death of Alphege, Archbishop of Canterbury, who was bludgeoned to death in Greenwich by Danish invaders led by Thrum in 1012. The body was left to rot unburied when the ransom money 'by the people of the Citie and Diocese' (of Canterbury) was not forthcoming, Lambarde, quoting from William of Malmesbury, recounts the less well-known medieval legend of the miraculous properties of the blood of the saint when the Danes suddenly 'perceived that a dead sticke, being annointed with his bloud, waxed suddently greene again, and began the next day to blossome'.

The Saint in the Tree

In 1242 a new house of Carmelites was founded in Kent at Aylesford where a Kentish man known as Simon Angelus or Simon Stock was chosen as general governor of the new order. Before joining the Whitefriars, who were transforming from an order of hermits to mendicant friars, St Simon had for many years lived as a hermit in a tree stump (or 'stock' – hence his name) and it was he who led the community in their new religious lifestyle and founded new houses in England, Ireland and Spain. The saint was given a vision of the Virgin Mary and his relics are held in the friary at Aylesford. Simon Stock has not been formerly canonised.

Inevitably a great number of saints simply disappeared with the Reformation – in churches their shrines were demolished, their images whitewashed and their statues removed and burnt along with their relics. Many saints' days were written out of the calendar and the *Legenda Aurea* was replaced by biblical text. The fabulous and entertaining stories were told no more – certainly too many of the 'lives' of the saints were patent fabrications – but the artistic loss to churches was irreparable.

A Puritan Postcript

In 1644, the Revd Richard Culmer, known by his parishioners as 'Blue Dick of Thanet' or 'Blueskin Dick' because he wore a blue hassock instead of the customary clerical black, caused consternation in Canterbury Cathedral when he smashed precious medieval windows originally donated by Edward IV, because he objected to their 'Romish' depiction of saints. Walter Jerrold in *Highways and Byways in Kent* recounts that when Culmer arrived at his first parish in Kent, his less than enthusiastic parishioners, fearing for their precious medieval glass, locked the church door and hid the key. Culmer's answer was to break a window in order to gain entry, whereupon he smashed every bit of medieval stained glass in the church after which he carefully effaced any decoration which took the shape of a cross.

1. Maypole Dance, Hadlow school, from around 1915. (Photo: Anne and Bill Hughes)

2. Hadlow School May Procession and May Queen, around 1913. (Photo: Anne and Bill Hughes)

3. The maypole dance at Dartford, *c.* 1896. (Photo: Fran and Geoff Doel Collection)

4. May Day celebrations (from Kent One Hundred Years Ago).

5. A Jack-in-the-Green at Lewisham May Day celebrations, 1890s. (Photo courtesy of the late Roy Judge)

6. Whitstable May Day celebrations with a Jack-in-the-Green, 1910.

7. Rochester Jack-in-the-Green, 1999. (Photo: Geoff Doel)

8. Whitstable Grotto (reproduced from A.G. Collard, The Oysters and Dredgers of Whitstable), 1902.

9. Mr Jorrocks morris at Sidmouth Folk Festival, 1987. (Photo courtesy of Mick Lynn)

10. The Hartley Morris at The Man of Kent pub, East Peckham, June 2002. (Photo: Geoff Doel)

11. Beating the Bounds, Rochester, *c.* 1910

12. Beating the Bounds, Canterbury.

13. Detail from a summons to the Horn Fair at Charlton. Headed 'A General Summons to all the Hornified Fumblers, To assemble at Horn Fair October 18', The handbill was printed by T. Batchelar of 115 Long Alley, Moorfields, London. People would dress up in drag and adorn horns and masks to attend this carnival of cuckoldry. (Courtesy of Roy Palmer)

14. Edenbridge Bonfire Society, 1928. (Archival photo courtesy of Dave Watts)

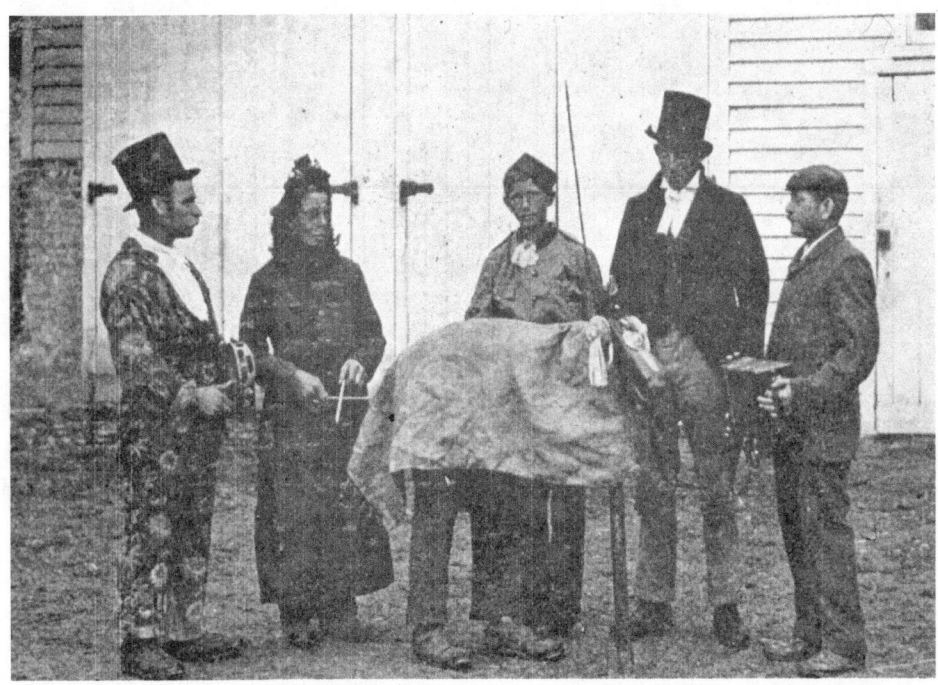

15. St Nicholas at Wade Hoodeners, 1905. Photo: Percy Maylam.

16. Tonbridge Hooden horse and waggoner Glenn Miller, 2001. (Photo: Geoff Doel)

17. Hooden horse convention, Marsh Gate Inn, 2000. (Photo: Geoff Doel)

18. Hooden horse from Maidstone Museum. (Photo: Geoff Doel, 1990)

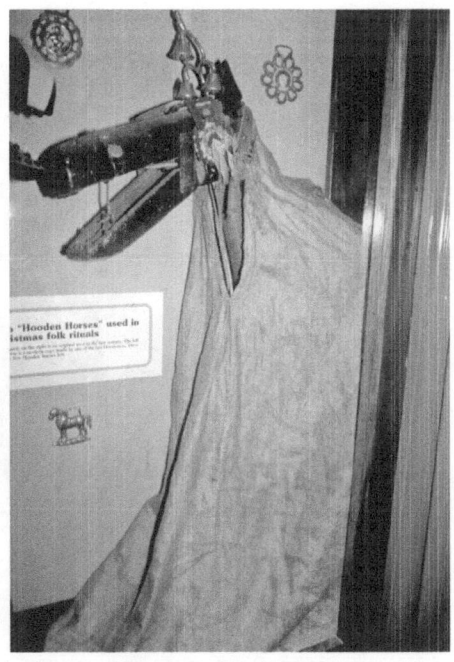

19. Hooden horse from. Folkestone Museum. The Folkestone Museum Hooden horses are now in the Deal Maritime Museum. (Photo: Geoff Doel, 1996)

20. Penshurst Place. (Photo: Geoff Doel)

21. The Tonbridge Mummers and Hoodeners at the Museum of Kent Life, Cob Tree, New Year's Day 1992. (Photo: Simon Evans)

22. 'Washing the children on a Sunday', a nineteenth-century image of hopper's tents.

23. Picking hops into a bin in the 1950s.

24. Hop-pickers on the road to Kent by 'Phiz'.

25. Hop-pickers resting by 'Phiz'.

26. The Hop-pickers Memorial, Hadlow churchyard. (Photo: Geoff Doel)

27. The church of St Mary, Reculver. (Lithograph by C. Hullmandell, 1822)

28. The death of Thomas à Becket.

29. St Dunstan tweaks the nose of the Devil with red-hot tongs.

30. The Black Prince's well, Harbledown. (Photo: Geoff Doel)

31. St Edith's Tomb, Kemsing. (Photo: Geoff Doel)

32. Mummers at Brenchley, *c.* 1920. Photo courtesy of Roundabout – the village magazine of Brenchley and Matfield.

33. The West Malling Champions, 1986. (Photo: Simon Evans)

34. Arden of Faversham

35. The Bearsted Play as performed by the Tonbridge Mummers, January 2003. (Photo: Doc Rowe)

36. The Tonbridge Mini-Mummers, Aylesford Priory, 1991. (Photo: Archie Turnbull)

37. The witch's frolic by George Cruikshank.

38. Kits Coty House, an early nineteenth-century print.

39. 'Thomas Ingoldsby' alias Richard Harris Barham, drawn by his son.

40. Old Nick comes to collect Dick (from the brothers of Birchington).

42. Bilsington Priory, reputed to be haunted.

43. Brookland church, June 1998. (Photo: Geoff Doel)

44. The Cardinal's Error, Tonbridge, 2002. (Photo: Geoff Doel)

45. The Cooper's Arms, Rochester, 2002. (Photo: Geoff Doel)

46. The Black Horse, Pluckley. (Photo: Geoff Doel)

47. The Ingoldsby House in Burgate Street, Canterbury.

48. St Nicholas' Hospital, Harbledown. (Photo: Geoff Doel)

49. Leeds Castle, by kind permission of the Leeds Castle Foundation.

50. The George and Dragon, Tonbridge, 2002. (Photo: Geoff Doel)

51 & 52. Above: Candidates for Watts' Poor Travellers, 1881.
Opposite: The Watts Charity building, Rochester, 2002. (Photo: Geoff Doel)

53. The Biddenden Maids.

54. The Biddenden village sign. (Photo: Geoff Doel)

55. Biddenden Dole, 1902. (Photo: Sir Benjamin Stone)

56. Biddenden Dole, 1984. (Photo: Geoff Doel)

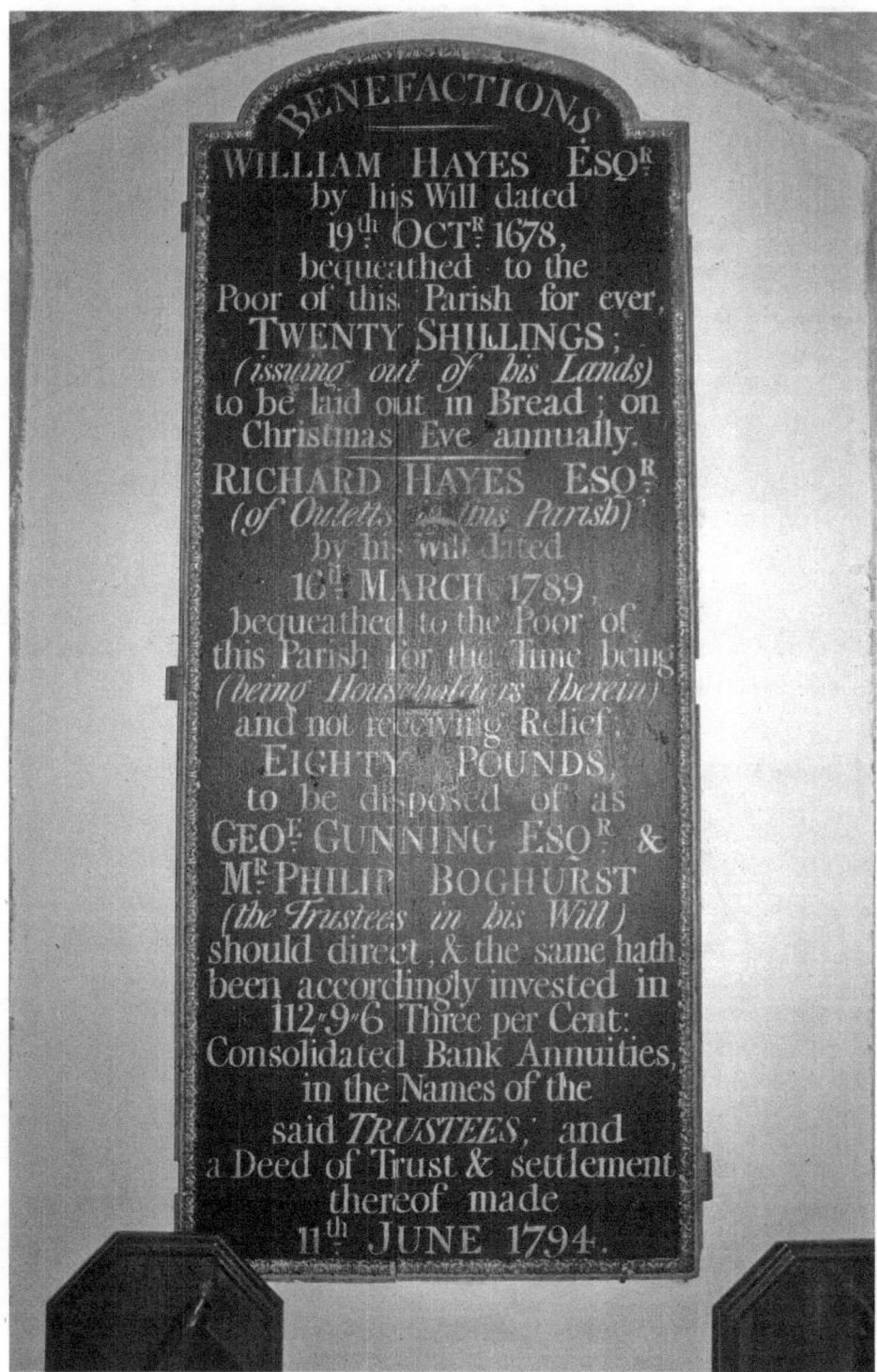

57. Bread Dole, Cobham church. (Photo: Geoff Doel)

6

PAGEANTS & STREET THEATRE

Kent is fortunate to have a number of surviving references to dramatic spectacle and ritual drama and its performances in the Middle Ages.

The Procession of the Boy Bishop

There were, for example, street processions of the Boy Bishop during the midwinter period, a popular custom dating from the late twelfth century and centring around the election of a 'Boy Bishop' from amongst young church choristers. The custom is known to have taken place in Rochester and Canterbury Cathedral School as well as in the collegiate church and a number of other parish churches in Kent, including New Romney, the latter appropriately dedicated to St Nicholas, the patron saint of children and our proto-Santa Claus. The election was probably held on 6 December (St Nicholas' Day) and was the prelude to a week-long series of activities known as the 'Feast of Boys'. The mini-bishop was dressed in full bishop's attire along with a mini mitre and crozier, all expensive items. After vespers on St John's Day (27 December) the boy bishop led a singing procession of choristers to the high altar, the latter dressed as the 'higher' clergy in silk copes and carrying candles. They were followed by the adult chapter. The boys then seated themselves in the stalls in the choir which were normally used by the men and their little 'Bishop', presumably in the most important seat, officiated at all the services except mass. Ronald Hutton in his book

The Stations of the Sun, claims that it was usual during this festival to have a candle-lit street procession of the little choristers, who sang as they processed, during which the little prelate 'blessed the spectators and collected money from them for parish funds'. A surviving reference to the New Romney 'Boy Bishop Procession' indicates that New Romney church took its procession to nearby Lydd. The custom was banned by Henry VIII in 1541.

The Procession of the Watch and the Pageant of the Martyrdom of St Thomas

A civic torchlight procession with its accompanying pageant for many years provided a colourful and dramatic spectacle for the citizens of the walled city of Canterbury in the late Middle Ages. The procession with its float took place on a July evening, on the eve of a public holiday, a Saint's Day marking the translation of the city's patron saint, St Thomas à Becket (July 10). A 'play', or it may have been a 'dumb show', was performed by boys and had as its subject matter a plot that needed no explanation to the audience and was appropriate to the religious feast day – the martyrdom of Archbishop Becket in his Cathedral at Canterbury. Many details of the procession are lacking. We do not know the route taken, and it may have varied every year, but the wagon may conceivably have paused outside the houses of important Canterbury burghers while the play was performed, or performed before the gates of friaries and religious houses and in the precincts of the Cathedral and the collegiate church.

Those who marched in the procession were the Constabulary or 'Watch' – an armed force who were responsible to the Canterbury City Fathers for the apprehension of vagrants and the keeping of the peace generally. In a book of the ordinances enacted by the Court of Burgmote dated to 1490, it is stated that the Watch marched in procession and in full uniform each carrying a lighted 'cresset' or torch. The procession was headed by the Sheriff of Canterbury on horseback with a mounted attendant, the former 'onestly emparelled', which probably indicates his sheriff's regalia and best robes, presumed to be scarlet and white as these were the city colours. The sheriff led the procession on horseback but closely behind rode the Mayor, in full mayoral robes and chain of office, followed by all of the city Aldermen, the Town Clerk and the 'Comen Counsel'. Any of these who chose not to attend was subject to a hefty fine. The dignitaries were on horseback; each carried two flares (bought at his own expense), and in the case of the Mayor, a number of additional torches. Accounts of the event indicate that the evening was splendidly noisy and with a quantity of music – a trumpeter advanced before the mounted officials and a drummer marched with the Watch, providing the beat to keep the constables marching in time

– the two musicians were paid 20d and 8d respectively for the evening's work. The London Waits (a professional or near-professional group of musicians) were also used to keep the audience entertained, for which they were paid the princely sum of 10s. Exploded gunpowder and volleys of gun shots by the Watch during the evening added to the excitement of the occasion. On one occasion two unfortunate 'Flemmings' who had only recently joined the constabulary were nearly blown up by a gunpowder explosion and were each given 6d in compensation.

The 'Pagent of Seynt Thomas' (Thomas à Becket being the patron of the city) became part of the Procession of the Watch either in 1503 or 1504. It was staged on a two-wheeled heavy wagon which may have been drawn by horses and there were men in attendance. The 'stage-set' represented the 'altar of the Sword's Point' in the Cathedral before which the martyrdom would be enacted.

The five actors were all children, perhaps choristers from the Benedictine monastery of *Corpus Christi*. The boy playing Becket was vested as a contemporary archbishop, the murderers wore helmets and flourished hired swords, and were dressed as contemporary knights. Once it was trundled to one of the pre-arranged points within the city of Canterbury, the wagon was halted and the martyrdom enacted before the citizens. The archbishop was surrounded as he knelt in prayer before the altar. Swords were flourished, clashed and brought down upon Thomas, who fell before the altar. One can imagine the gusto with which the boy actors struck the one playing Thomas over and over again with their swords. Under the altar, a hidden child provided with bags full of animal blood squirted the liquid through slits in the altar hangings. That gave the Watch the signal for gunpowder to be set off with a massive bang, during which confusion a wooden contraption was rapidly set in motion representing an angel with flapping wings whirling round a pole to which it was attached by wire (a possible indication that Thomas's soul ascended straight to heaven). The 'contraption' was worked by yet another child hidden under the capacious altar. The wagon was then trundled away, no doubt to great applause, while the boys adopted their original poses in a *tableau vivant*.

When not in use the pageant wagon was kept in the female Priory of St Sepulchre for several years until transferred to the disused Archbishop's palace in 1515.

By 1541 the city had erased the image of Becket from their seals as the king, Henry VIII, had confiscated the entire wealth of Canterbury Cathedral and, it was commonly rumoured, had had Becket's bones fired from a cannon. It was therefore judged prudent to replace the religious pageant with a secular subject. Imitating London's Gog and Magog Procession, an alternative and apparently very well-received procession of 'Gyaunts' (giants) accompanied the Watch. In 1553 Mary, a Catholic, was on the throne, and for a few years the Pageant of St Thomas was revived to accompany the Watch. A new pageant wagon was made, larger than the first, as the old one had been sold in 1537. New clothes were made for the child actors and numerous torches and candlesticks provided for its illumination. But the simple belief and the uncritical enjoyment had dissipated – this time there was no whirling angel, no spurting blood, no gunpowder explosions. When Elizabeth I came to the throne, the pageant was suppressed as part of the procession of the Watch.

The Lydd Passion Play

It is now thought that in many Kentish parishes, religious and other kinds of drama were regularly enacted on parcels of land which in the Middle Ages were called the village 'pleystoles'.

Archival records of dramatic activity in the town of Lydd in the late Midde Ages, fragmented as they are, indicate that this little town on the edges of the Romney marshes enjoyed regular visits in the late Middle Ages from pre-invited professional acting troupes and musicians as well as from touring bands of itinerant players. Lydd also had its own religious play sponsored by the town, *The Interlude of Our Lord's Passion*, a dramatic re-enactment of the events which led to Christ's death, performed in English, with the gospel text extended to include secular and comic episodes. The parts of Jesus, Mary, Herod, Pontius Pilate etc., were all performed by a local men-only team drawn from fraternities connected with the local churches. Elected 'Wardens of the Plays', some of whom were local priests, were in charge of the monetary remuneration including the 'bred, wine and bere' which were payments for rehearsals and performances, as well as all necessary costumes, props and machinery. Although the text (which would have been known as 'the Playboke') does not survive, it would have been kept by someone in authority, such as the Common Clerk. The play was performed within the 'pleystole' and on a scaffold on a number of Sundays (perhaps as a preface to the Easter celebration and at Whitsuntide) and is known to have been played elsewhere in Kent. The number of performances in Lydd might indicate that it proved a popular 'draw' and that audiences were being drawn from nearby hamlets and villages, augmenting that of the parish church.

The neighbouring town of New Romney, which like Lydd had played host to numbers of acting troupes, eventually formed its own copy-cat acting troupe in 1463, with six fraternities attached to its two churches and two chapels furnishing the actors. One Agnes Ford was paid 6s 8d to write the text.

'The May'

Records indicate that Lydd's acting troupe performed another play or pageant every year in the late Middle Ages though all that remains of this is its title – *The May* – with accounts for the years 1442-44. There is the possibility that this was the community's celebration of the advent of summer or 'the summer games', when greenery was brought in from the woods to decorate the town or village. Some communities had an elected 'Summer Lord' (often called 'Robin Hood') and a 'May Queen' or 'Marian' (thought to be a man in appropriate costume) who on May Day led the company in a rowdy procession through the streets, after which they took their places in a specially erected 'green bower' while 'may games', music, dancing, wrestling and archery contests were performed 'in their honour'. If a village or town had a morris team, they were inevitably present. The 'summer games' had a general reputation for drunkenness for these were the summer 'ales' where beer was sold for fund raising. Accounts for 1432 indicate that two gallons of wine were delivered to the Lydd 'players', 'when they 'showed their May' which indicates that they were paid well for their efforts.

The Play of 'St George'

The cult of St George became popular and more widespread during the Crusades after Richard the Lionheart placed his English army under that saint's protection. In the late Middle Ages the saint's life, particularly his legendary rescue of a king's daughter from a fire-breathing dragon, became well known through *The Golden Legend* which Caxton had translated and printed. The Lydd players are known to have performed an enactment of this combat on the saint's feast day every April.

Arden of Faversham

On 24 March 1551, Alison Arden, the wife of Thomas Arden, Comptroller of HM's Customs, was publicly burnt alive in Canterbury for masterminding her husband's death in his own home at Faversham. Also implicated was her lover, Mosbie, Arden's servants and 'two desperate ruffians' named Blackwill and Shakebag. Retribution was swift once the offenders were seized. Two were hung in chains to starve to death, one at Faversham, the other near Ospringe, three others ended their lives on the gallows, and Alice's woman servant, loyal to her mistress throughout, was burned to death before a crowd at Faversham.

It is unique at this date that a domestic murder could be deemed of such dramatic potential and fascination that it became the subject of a play and in this form carried before the people and enacted in private halls, inn yards, private theatres, perhaps even at the royal court. Though the playwright remains anonymous, in the past this play of *Arden of Faversham, his true and lamentable Tragedy* was regularly, though wrongly, attributed to Shakespeare. It was written in 1592, during the reign of Elizabeth I, possibly drawing from Holinshed's vivid account of the event in which he claims that no less than six attempts were made on Arden's life before he was finally stabbed to death by his 'disloyal and wanton' wife. Ironically, recent scholarship suggests that although the husband is portrayed in the play and in Holinshed as a thoroughly estimable, even noble character, the reality was quite different. Thomas Arden was a man subject to violent mood swings, and a sadistic and regular wife-beater.

The Seven Champions

Plays of the Seven Champions are the Kent terms for Mummers plays – short, ritualistic midwinter plays performed by males with traditional words and costumes. They feature a Father Christmas, two boasting champions who fight, one being killed and – in a ritualistic sequence – revived by a mysterious, well-travelled and socially superior Doctor. Various begging characters then ask for money – usually Johnny Jack ('wife and family on my back') and Beelzebub in the Kent versions. There seems to be a symbolic or sympathetic magic connection with the life-force and/or passing of the seasons at the Midwinter period. The academic world is generally agreed that the evolution of these plays through village communities has links with the pattern of the development of European drama from religious and ritualistic origins. But many folklorists (perhaps lacking a background in medieval drama) still become hysterical at the suggestion of anything but a purely sociological and quite recent origin. Textual evidence and characterisation point to at least a Tudor provenance, with probable earlier – possibly miming – elements incorporated.

Mummers' plays were common in rural areas in many parts of England; they are rare in eastern coastal regions and the east coast of Kent is no exception, preferring the Hooden Horse midwinter ritual (see chapter two). But seven more or less complete texts survive from West Kent villages and small towns and text fragments and memories of many more. In the appendix we have given an example of the earliest West Kent text collected, that from Shoreham as performed in the 1890s, taken down from dictation from Mr W.J. Atkinson of Rolvenden, who took part in the play whilst a boy living in Shoreham. The text differs a little (with one different character) from that still performed by the Darenth Valley Champions, put together from valuable oral, tape-recorded research in the 1970s by Simon Evans, Charlie Jacobs, Terry Heaslip and others into the fascinating group of Seven Champion Plays from the Darenth Valley. Those interviewed were performers from just before the First World War, some twenty years after Mr Atkinson's text.

The Darenth Valley runs from near Westerham to Dartford and so far four distinct Mummers plays have been discovered in villages through which the river flows – Brasted, Riverhead, Shoreham and Sutton-at-Hone. The Mummers sides were known as 'The Seven Champions' or 'Christmas Champions' and mumming was often referred to as 'championing'. Simon, Charlie and Terry's researches indicate face-blacking and paper costumes and a December season of performances starting with big houses and then concentrating on pubs in the run-up to Christmas.

In 1974 Annis Cumfrey, daughter of a Brasted butcher, researched her family's memories of the Brasted Play of the Seven Champions for Mollie Glenn, a teacher at Westerham School, later giving details in an article for *Bygone Kent*. Her elder sisters remembered the Mummers from about 1910-1915 and their father saying 'Here come the Champions' as they marched up the street and providing beer for them when they performed in the kitchen and scullery. The last performance they remembered was a shortened production with fewer characters in 1922. Jim Pattenden played the part of Father Christmas and his brother Jack took the begging part of Little Johnny Jack with 'dolls sewn onto the back of his costume' and the lines:

> Here comes I, Little Johnny Jack,
> My wife and family at my back.
> My family is large and I am small,
> And every little helps us all

Other parts included King George, Turkish Knight, the Turk's Mother and the Doctor, who was able to cure 'pains within and pains without'. This led to researcher Simon Evans meeting three surviving Brasted Mummers, including Jack Pattenden from whom he took down the complete text, which has formed the basis of a spirited revival of the play for many years by 'The Darenth Valley Champions' (still extant), and many anecdotes. One story gives an intriguing example of textual change in the oral tradition. After the Turkish Knight was slain by King George, the Turk's Mother spoke the lines:

> Is there a Doctor to be found,
> To cure this man who lies bleeding on the ground?

This was changed to 'to cure this man who lies bleeding in my arms' which, according to Jack 'put a stop to us having to lie on the floor spoiling our clothes' (though there is also a tradition of paper costumes being used in the village). Annis Cumfrey's sisters' recollections of the dolls being sewn to Johnny Jack's costume could indicate that ribbon costumes were sometimes used (as elsewhere).

The Brasted Champions are known to have performed at Toys Hill, Ide Hill, Westerham and Sundridge and included visits to several large houses. The Shoreham Champions visited pubs in Shoreham, Otford, Eynsford and Bat and Ball; their costumes were ribbons sewn onto old clothes. Texts for Riverhead and Sutton-at-Hone (the latter was performed for many years by Wadard Morris and has recently been revived by the Canterbury Mummers and Hoodeners) were collected, but with little background information. The text of the Leigh Combat Play, performed in the village near Tonbridge south of the Darenth Valley, is actually one of the Darenth Valley plays and taken to Leigh by an émigré.

Mummers were remembered performing at a Plaxtol venue or venues in the late 1880s, where they were rewarded with 'home-made wine, cakes and sweetmeats'. Some wore soldiers' attire, and a couplet from the speech of the Doctor has been preserved:

> I can cure your pains within or without,
> And also I can give you some pills for the gout.

The Medway Valley is another focal point for mumming plays. Regular traditional performances of the West Malling Mummers Play survived remarkably late – into the 1930s. Local interest has helped in the preservation of enough of the list of characters, text and costume details to enable a very lively revival of the tradition from the 1980s and still going strong by a team organised by Alan Austen, a Malling folklorist, singer, musician and morris dancer. The play is performed on the Saturday evening before Christmas, when most of the local hostelries are visited and about eight performances given.

Anthony Cronk in his *A Short History of West Malling* (1951) mentions the play:

> Then at Christmastide, there was the genuine West Malling folk-play, 'The Seven Champions', which was regularly performed by local stalwarts right up until 1930, the players travelling round the taverns and private houses in the same manner as carol singers... The actors wore outlandish costume, and all had blackened faces except St George, who wore a brass helmet with a plume resembling that of a life-guardsman.

Anthony Cronk printed a typical Mummers text in his book which he does not claim to be the actual West Malling text, but which has a number of distinctive Kentish mumming features, with additional elements drawn from the 'universal' text put together by E.K. Chambers in his *The English Folk Play*. The best guess is that Cronk had obtained parts of the genuine West Malling Play and filled in the gaps from Chambers.

The Honorary Secretary of the Rotary Club of Malling, Mr J.A. Dawson, wrote to Alan Austen about the play in 1982:

> I was able to recall the Mummers at West Malling... about 1912 or 1913. My memory is of about four players dressed in highly coloured military uniforms which probably came from the Boer War era. They would visit houses just before Christmas and have sham sword fights outside the front doors of houses with much worthy shouting conversation of which in my youthful eight years I could not understand a word.

We recently met a gentleman whose father had performed in the Yalding Play and there was a Rochester play, seen by the young Russell Thorndike, who based the Mummers play in 'Doctor Syn' at Lympe Castle on it. The Rochester historian Edwin Harris saw the Rochester play in the Queen Charlotte public house opposite his house:

> Their performance consisted in each reciting some doggerel, winding up with a sword fight. Some of the champions are wounded and the doctor, coming to their aid, performs a short and wonderful cure, whereon a collection is made and the Seven Champions move on to the next licensed house and repeat the performance.

A lady we met in the early 1990s remembered her father, a Mr Martin who lived at Gillingham as a young man, reciting these lines to his family:

Here comes I old Beelzebub,
On my head I carry my tub,
In my hand my frying pan
Don't you think I'm a funny old man?

Are these lines from a lost Gillingham play? The Beelzebub is a distinctive feature of Kent plays.

The Bearsted Play is well documented, though as with the Shoreham play there are textual variations. The Bearsted Play is referred to in Chamber's List of Texts in *The English Folk Play* as being in a 'MS of Miss Coombes'. *A History of Bearsted and Thurnham* (1939) quotes a booklet dealing with village traditions including the annual appearance of the Seven Champions in earlier days:

Another event was the appearance of the Seven Champions just before Christmas. They would appear dressed in paper to suit the part and recite such strains as "I'm little Jack Sweep, all the money I get I keep" and "Here I come, Beelzebub! In my hand I carry a club, in my hand a dripping pan, don't you think I'm a jolly man". The words would be followed by the beating of the pan with the Club and we hope the money gained covered the depreciation of the utensils.

The lines quoted refer to the two 'begging' characters that come on at the end of the play, Jack Sweep and Beelzebub. The surviving text of Bearsted has an almost identical Beelzebub speech, but a different one for Jack Sweep:

In comes I, Jack Sweep,
All these men I have to keep,
Whether they're little or whether they're tall,
It takes a lot of money to keep them all.
It's money I want and money I crave,
If you don't give me money
I'll sweep you all into your grave.

The opening lines are closer to a Little Johnny Jack character, whilst the earlier quoted speech for Jack is similar to the lines of the unique Chimney Sweep character at West Malling.

The manuscript of Bearsted mentioned by Chambers disappeared, but Carl Willets advertised in the *Kent Messenger* and was sent a copy of the play formerly acted at Bearsted School between the wars. This has the unusual feature of beginning with a sweeping figures – 'Rock' the Gardener with a besom broom:

Open the door and let me in.
I beg your pardon, I'm sure to win.
Whether we rise or whether we fall
Room, room, room I require.
Step in guard, and show your face like fire.

Another sweeper, Jack Sweep, enters near the end:

In comes I Jack Sweep.
All the men I have to keep
Whether they're little or whether they're tall,
It takes a lot o'money to keep them all.

Followed by Beelzebub and, again unusually, ending with Father Christmas with the lines:

> In comes I old Father Christmas.
> Am I welcome or am I not?
> Hope Father Christmas is not forgot.

This makes eight characters for the Seven Champions Play and it looks as if the Gardener has been added. The Tonbridge Mummers have revived this play with Father Christmas as the opening character.

Parts of a Tonbridge Mummers play are recorded from the Edwardian period, said to be a well established tradition going back at least a hundred years before that, with costumes handed down. From two weeks before Christmas the Tonbridge Mummers toured many of the big houses in the area, including Fairlawne and Somerhill reached on foot, followed by pub performances. The seven characters included Father Christmas, King George III, Turkish Knight, Prince of Wales, Doctor and Bull Slasher (presumably a corruption of Bold Slasher). Ernie Chandler played Father Christmas and introduced the play with the lines:

> Here I come, old Father Christmas,
> Am I welcome or am I not?

The Prince dared the Turk (played by George Hayward);

> O Turk, O Turk, O do not caper,
> Or I'll mow thee down with my long taper!

The Turk stabbed the Prince, who was revived by the Doctor arriving with 'all sorts of cures', played by Leslie Kinchin. A Rottingdean play also features The Prince Regent, but it is unusual in Sussex and Kent for the Turkish Knight to win the battle.

The Milton Regis Play was discovered by Carl Willetts who supplied details to the *Roomer* magazine. Most of the details come from a former Milton postmaster, Douglas Knowles. Carl comments in his article:

> The play was performed by workers from local brickfields to earn beer money at Christmas, the last performance being in 1904. At that time there were at least five brickfields in the area… According to Mr Knowles:
>
>> People used to look forward to the Christmas tour, the players added
>> a lot of their own words to the original play. They were very amusing

characters. They used to visit about three pubs in the High Street each night and would do the odd charity show in the hall.

The Doctor of the last performance, Bill Crook, gave Mr Knowles a handwritten copy of the play in about 1961, and showed Mr Knowles a photograph of the actors; the whereabouts of this photograph are now unknown.

Recently a photograph from around 1920 of what seems to be a double Mumming team (that is with characters duplicated) has come to light from Brenchley. This is the only archival Mummers photograph we know of from Kent and we have included it in this book, courtesy of the *Brenchley and Matfield Magazine*.

All plays so far mentioned are from west Kent. There is one east Kent play from Dover, in the late nineteenth-century *Ordish Collection*, and it is controversial. In another book we were careful to state that: 'This text was supplied by a butler and seems to be an intriguing *mixture* of Kent traditional texts and "pace egg" texts' (pace egg plays are Easter Mumming Plays from the Pennine and Lake District region). While researching the *Ordish Collection*, Geoff advised Steve Roud, the then Librarian of the Folklore Society, that the Dover play was a hybrid text, with 'pace egg' features in addition to its evident Kentish elements. We were therefore surprised to read in his critical review of our book that this play is not uniquely Kentish because of its 'Northern "Pace-Egg Play" features' – a fact which we had already made crystal clear. We contend that while the chronological table and regional identity is of the utmost importance, mummers' plays which are organic and never devised as reading matter and whose original 'texts' have not survived, cannot be reduced to a limp consensus. Therefore 'bastard' texts such as the Dover Play should always be considered as playing a possible and legitimate part in the evolution of this kind of dramatic tradition.

A close comparison of the Dover Play with the Bearsted and Milton texts and other Kent and Sussex texts reveals some distinctly local features, particularly in the words of the Doctor, Devil Doubt and Beelzebub. We think an open mind should be kept on the possibility of this play being performed locally as its classification in the Ordish manuscript suggests, or at least as incorporating Kentish elements particularly in the latter half of the play.

Meanwhile the Mumming tradition in Kent is being kept alive by The West Malling Mummers, the Tonbridge Mummers, the Hartley Morris, the Darent Valley Champions and Bishop Gundulph's Mummers. Long may they thrive!

7

THINGS UNHOLY
SUPERSTITION & WITCHCRAFT

Keith Thomas, in his book *Religion and the Decline of Magic*, believes that many superstitions and superstitious practices are linked to the religious practices of pre-Reformation days. Certainly many items such as holy water and church candles were often procured or secreted from churches and used by people in the late Middle Ages in a superstitious way. Holy water was scattered on the fields to help the crops grow, or drunk as a remedy for sickness, the orthodox view, being that 'there was nothing improper about such actions provided that they were performed out of a genuine Christian faith'. From letters written in the time of Henry VIII, we have examples of a Kent vicar with a parish in Bethersden advising sick parishioners to drink holy water as a medicine, while another letter describes how citizens in Canterbury ran to church during a raging storm for holy water to sprinkle inside their houses.

Conjurors and 'Wise Women'

Depositions made in connection with the prosecution of 'white witches' and wizards (also known as 'conjurors' or 'cunning men') brought to the attention of archbishops during their visitations or taken before secular and ecclesiastical courts in Kent indicate that, throughout the Middle Ages, 'wise women' and conjurors or wizards were regularly applied to, mainly by the superstitious, illiterate and the poor, who believed in their spells, charms and magic techniques. During the Kentish visitations of Archbishop Warham just prior to the Reformation, the prelate was informed of an old woman at Stone who used a stick she had named 'Moses Yard' to bless beasts and to cure children of the worms. Both 'wise women' and conjurors were regularly applied to for 'charming' warts and healing, but they had other abilities and functions.

A cunning man could for example detect or name a thief in the community, and suggest where stolen goods might be recovered. The apparatus for this was so simple — a sieve used in conjunction with shears — or a key dangled on a string over a Bible — that Reginald Scot (1538-1599) could claim ironically that not only did every Kentish parish have its miracle worker, 'some had seventeen or eighteen', an indication that many were tempted to practise magic in the Kent countryside.

Some conjuror's spells were written up in books. In 1610, William Lawse, a clerk in Halden, returned from work one day to find his cattle injured and some corn stolen. With his friend, William Childes, a weaver at Bethersden, and with a third man, they consulted a 'conjuring book' to see if the names of the perpetrators could be found. Following 'directions', they drew a large chalk circle on the floor with Latin words inside the circle. The third friend then read certain Psalms while Childes chanted 'I exorcise and conjure thee' (from *Records of Maidstone*, Maidstone, 1926). Unsurprisingly, the spell proved ineffectual, the culprit was not found, and the men were accused of practising witchcraft.

Many Kent farmers, fearing an early frost, excessive rain or an over-long winter, are known to have consulted cunning men to forecast the weather and coming harvest. To do this, the wizards (no doubt after some payment was offered) looked into the future by means of a crystal ball, or 'scryed', that is observed the patternings of egg white dropped into water or of ink spilt on to some smooth surface. Others could forecast the future of individuals by means of a 'familiar spirit' that instructed them.

One conjuror, Robert Harris, in 1556 was claimed to have 'worked great feats of divination' in Maidstone the county town of Kent, simply by observing his client's face.

In 1590, an itinerant quack doctor who had gained a popular reputation for sorcery, Thomas Fansome, was apprehended by the High Commission in the Diocese of Canterbury and brought before the court. He confessed to selling love charms (papers on which there were 'magical writings') and casting horoscopes. His usual fee appears to have been 6s 8d, although he was occasionally 'paid in kind', accepting, it was said, a gold ring and two 'half-kirtles'. His deposition is of interest in that he was consulted not just by the lower classes; he cast one spell, for example for a lady, so that 'my Lord Dover' would 'look favourably on her husband'.

Keith Thomas suggests that conjurors such as Harris and Fansome were able to maintain their prestige 'by a combination of fraud and good psychology' as much as by magical practices.

The Emergence of the Witch

As the late medieval church had admitted the existence and practice of witchcraft, and the law provided for the punishment of witchcraft when it harmed humans, the persecution of witches inevitably increased when handbooks became available. Some of these emanated from or were inspired by European texts which claimed to codify practices drawn from the torture and confessions of witches on the continent. Witches were increasingly being identified not just with herbal spells and primitive sympathetic magic but with devil worship, pacts, familiars, covens and formidable magical and malignant powers. However, not everyone was persuaded of these powers.

One such man was Reginald Scot, a Kentish squire who lived in the age of Elizabeth I. He inherited and farmed lands in Smeeth and was MP for New Romney. He had personally witnessed scores of trials and punishments of men and women who had been indicted for witchcraft in courts of law in country districts in Kent. Scot, who had been schooled at Oxford (although he left without taking his degree), had a healthy scepticism of the fabulous powers that so-called witches were supposed to possess. He was also aware of how susceptible poor (and often senile) old women were to fraudulent accusations. Scot quotes the Vicar of Brenchley who had publicly declared that his sore throat was the result of a spell worked by an old 'hag' in his parish, and adds drily that the clergyman's parishioners were equally persuaded that it was 'the French Pox' (syphilis).

In 1584 Scot produced an influential book – though it was rejected by fanatics and James I ordered it to be burnt – an impressive review of fashionable contemporary beliefs about witches and witchcraft, *The Discoverie of Witchcraft, wherein the lewd dealing of witches and witchmongers is notability detected, in sixteen books, where unto is added a treatise upon the nature and substance of spirits*. In this Scot suggested that the fascination with the persecution of witches should be rejected by all right-thinking men on the grounds of common sense and religion.

Scot believed that superstitious practices such as the use of holy candles in the utilisation of spell-making was little more than a debased residue of religious practices inherited from Roman Catholicism – 'The papists do it without shame, the others (conjurors, 'wise women') do it hugger mugger, secretly'. Scott genuinely considered that the majority of accused men and women brought before a court were totally innocent. He was aware, however, and in this he based his conclusions on the researches of Johan Weyer, a physician with whose work he was familiar, that some actually believed themselves to be witches with special powers to do harm. These were, Scot felt, deluded, possibly mentally ill, and in some cases, insane.

Scot was also alert to the way in which confessions were extracted from anyone reported to the authorities as an alleged witch. The procedure was not normally recorded. Many were beaten and deprived of sleep over a period of days by being 'walked' by a relay of helpers. Leading questions were asked until a confession was extracted. The witch was stripped naked – a humiliating process, for even the anus and sexual organs were searched – in order to find the 'devil's mark' – a supernumerary nipple, or pimple, wart or growth which the devil or grotesque 'familiar' could suckle from. All the suspects were asked leading questions regarding whether they could survive 'swimming' – which was often used as an option when deciding if a woman was a witch or not. This involved tying the suspect's arms to her feet with rope in front of her body, and throwing her into a flowing river or deep pond. The 'witch' would have a rope round her waist so that the body could be retrieved after the event. If the woman drowned she was declared innocent. Anyone who floated was declared a witch and brought out to be hanged or burned.

Breaking the Witch's Spell

One of the greatest services a white witch or conjuror could render in his community was to break a witch's spell. Scratching a witch or drawing her blood with a pin, needle or knife was thought to be an infallible means of arresting a spell. In 1593, a cunning man from Hastings known as Zacharias was consulted by anxious parents who believed that their sick child had been bewitched by a neighbour, 'Mother' Rogers. Zacharias' advice was unusual in that instead of recommending the usual pin thrust into an arm or body, he suggested the 'witch' should have a knife inserted into her buttocks. This is a good example of how the community, when dealing with such a feared and emotive subject as witchcraft, could often take the law into their own hands and administer rough justice without recourse to the law.

A white witch, Mother Baker of New Romney, was consulted when a child fell ill. The witch informed the parents that one of their neighbours had made 'a wax doll' which was harming the child. 'Dolls' or 'poupees' were made of butter or wax or were small, crudely carved, wooden effigies which could be stuffed with pins and burned and were often used by country people or witches as a means to harm others. Animal hearts were used in the same way, either to harm, or if stuffed up the chimney, as a means of combating witches' spells. When the parents of the ailing child searched the neighbour's house no such items were found. Later on, Mother Baker was observed secreting an animal heart on the so-called witch's property and was indicted for fraud.

Possession

There are a number of accounts in Kent of young women displaying symptoms of hystero-epilepsy. During the Middle Ages this was perceived as an example of demonic possession. Thomas says of most cases of possession that they were usually young women engaged in hysterical reaction against the religious disciplines or repression to which they had been subject (Thomas, *Religion*, p. 572). Early in 1574, the seventeen-year-old illegitimate daughter of a servant called Alice who served William Spooner of Westwell, Kent, began to manifest all the symptoms of 'possession'. One can imagine the excitement of the crowd that gathered on 13 October 1574, to cast out her devils. Four men held her down while she was interrogated. For two hours she resisted, gnashing her teeth, screaming, contorting her face and body. Finally she revealed the source of her bewitchment – an old woman with the same name as her mother who lived locally. She claimed that Satan lived in two bottles which were concealed in the old witch's house and that they had been used to bewitch certain villagers and to kill others. The crowd dispersed and ransacked old Alice's house. Someone discovered a single bottle under the back of old Alice's wall. Sadly, the records are incomplete and we do not know what action was taken and if old Alice was reprieved.

Practitioners of Witchcraft

Many villagers practised witchcraft in secret and did not consider themselves to be witches. Ewen recounts how in 1543, a Canterbury townswoman named Joanna Meriwether – who otherwise made no claims to being a witch – confessed to having cast a spell on a young woman Elizabeth Celsay and her mother with a holy candle. Confessions were often obtained from suspects over a number of days through beatings and sleep deprivation. Meriwether ultimately admitted that she had built a small fire over Elizabeth's faeces and allowed wax from a burning church candle to drip over it. She had later told neighbours (it is not clear if they were called as witnesses) that this would cause the 'girl's buttocks to divide into two parts'.

In 1993 some seventeenth-century jars were discovered, secreted up the chimneys of two cottages in High St Charing. Their inclusions (iron, hair, pins and strips of textile) would suggest that these were early seventeenth century counter-spells to combat witchcraft.

The Witch's Mark and Familiar

A common feature of English witch trials was the search for 'the Devil's mark', this (a wart, bruise, spot or extra nipple) would be recognisable as it could not bleed when cut. It was almost standard procedure for the accused to have pins and knives pushed into their heads and arms to see if blood could be drawn which ought to have proved them innocent but rarely did. The fact that no blood was produced may seem miraculous but was in some cases apparently due to special knives with retractable blades being used. Certainly suspects were publicly and humiliatingly searched for 'the Devil's mark'. In the so-called Maidstone witch trial of 1652, a growth was found under 'the witch' Mary Reade's tongue which she had to exhibit to the court as a mark of her guilt. It may have been because of the humiliation of such a search that another of the Maidstone 'witches', Anne Ashby, became hysterical with fear and fell into a fit, swelling into 'a monstrous and vast bigness'.

Linked with this belief in the Devil's mark was the idea of a familiar – an imp or devil – who suckled from the mark as from a teat. If an accused woman did not admit to having a familiar 'it became a common procedure in witch detection to isolate the suspect and wait for some animal or insect to appear as proof of her guilt' (Thomas, *Religion*, p. 530). Of the four 'Faversham witches' who were tried together in the seventeenth century, Joan Walliford admitted that her pet dog was her familiar and Jane Hott, who had steadfastly refused to admit she was a witch, finally broke down and confessed that 'something like a hedgehog' had suckled at her breast. Elizabeth Harris admitted that the Devil appeared as a mouse that returned to suckle every three or four days and Jan Cariden claimed that a shaggy, black dog came to her to suckle. These four women had landed in gaol because an affluent neighbour, Thomas Gardner, had fallen out of a window and landed on his behind. The mirth of passers-by had enraged him and he indicted the four as witches. After lengthy interrogations (and undoubted ill treatment) all four were sentenced to death though only three are recorded as having been put to death. Elizabeth's execution was postponed and it is possible that she may have been reprieved.

The Royal Witch

In the fifteenth century a number of illustrious personages were accused of witchcraft in Kent, probably as a means of discrediting them publicly and removing them from the political scene. One such was Joan of Navarre (1370-1437), widow of Henry IV who was accused by her step-son, Henry V, of practising witchcraft. Joan was found guilty and imprisoned for three years, part of that exile spent in Leeds Castle. Another royal woman tried for 'sorcery and witchcraft' in the chapel of this castle was Eleanor Duchess of Gloucester; her trial conducted by Archbishop Henry Chichele in 1440.

The Holy Maid of Kent

It is of course ironic that the most celebrated Kentish 'witch' was Elizabeth Barton, the 'Holy Maid of Kent', a young nun who was brought to trial on specious allegations of witchcraft in 1534, and was found guilty. Elizabeth was probably a liar and an exhibitionist – but witchcraft was a trumped-up charge and her death a foregone conclusion occasioned by political necessity.

As a young unlettered girl Elizabeth worked as a servant for Thomas Cobb, steward of the Archbishop of Canterbury's estates and hunting forest at Aldington. When she was sixteen Elizabeth experienced a series of spectacular fits, sixteen in all, after which she fell into a trance which lasted for days. The parish priest, Richard Masters, was able to vouch for her piety and called in Archbishop Warham of Canterbury. As a result of this Warham (at that point involved in rancorous debates on the pending divorce between Henry VIII and his wife, Catherine of Aragon) sent two Canterbury monks, Dr Bocking and Dan William Hadley from Christ Church to question and, it is suggested, possibly 'groom' and instruct her. More trances followed during which Elizabeth claimed to see the Virgin Mary, even producing a gilded letter from Mary Magdalen 'written in heaven'. More followed – Elizabeth spoke 'prophetically' of the hell-fire pains waiting for those who acted contrary to God's commandments (interpreted as a reference to Henry's urgent insistence on a marriage with Anne Boleyn).

On 15 August 1525, Elizabeth was 'cured' at a public ceremony staged before an invited audience of 2,000 including Sir Thomas More.

Elizabeth had been instructed by the Virgin that she 'would never take health of her body till such time as she had visited the image of Our Lady' at Court-at-Street, a Kentish chapel. Elizabeth was carried into the chapel on a litter 'her face wondrously disfigured, a voice speaking in her belly' and, in a three-hour trance, making numbers of prophecies regarding the joys of heaven and the pains of hell. She concluded by saying that the Virgin had instructed her to become a nun in the Priory of St Sulpice in Canterbury. After this astonishing performance, Elizabeth was pronounced 'cured'. Court chapel subsequently became a place of pilgrimage. Dr Bocking became her confessor and director in St Sulpice, and during the three years in which she was a professed nun, Elizabeth continued to make regular prophecies forecasting doom if Henry married Anne Boleyn.

Elizabeth was brought before Cranmer the Archbishop of Canterbury in July 1533. The details of her interrogation are unknown but she was declared a witch and sentenced to death. She made a voluntary confession at the trial in which she maintained:

> I am not so much to be blamed, considering that it was well known unto these learned men that I was a poor wench without learning... But because the things which I feigned were profitable unto them, therefore they much praised me, and bare me in hand that it was the Holy Ghost and not I that did them. And I, being puffed up with their praises fell into a proud and foolish fantasy with myself, and thought I might feign what I would.

The maid was hanged as a witch at Tyburn on 21 April 1534. Also hanged were Bocking, her former parish priest and several friars.

8

LEGENDS & GHOST LORE

In folklore it was common for prehistoric structures, such as megalithic tombs and stone circles, which were inexplicable to later cultures, to become associated with their gods and heroes as supernatural or superhuman manifestations. Thus prehistoric monuments in the Kentish landscape have been explained since Anglo-Saxon times through to Tudor and later antiquarians as being burial sites or cenotaphs to fallen chieftains and it can be difficult to disentangle folklore from antiquarian suggestions. An example is Juliberrie's Grave, a 144-foot prehistoric long barrow on the downs above Godmersham Park, of which Richard Gough in his 1806 edition of *Camden's Britannia* (which gives a fairly close rendition of the original Latin) states:

> Below (Chilham) is a tumulus covered with green turf, under which they say was buried many ages since 'Jullaber', whom some fancy a giant, others a witch. For myself, as I think some antient memorial is concealed under this name, I am almost persuaded that Laberius Durus the military tribune was buried here, having been slain by the Britons.

This seems to highlight a conflict between local folklore, which places Juliberrie as a giant or witch, and the antiquarian ideas of Camden, Lambarde and their later followers such as Gough who link the site (partly by name association) with the death of a Roman general in Britain mentioned by Caesar. Interestingly, Roman artefacts (though of the third century) were found with the skeletons in this barrow and preserved at Chilham Castle.

Prehistoric structures form the legendary burial sites of chieftains from both sides of the fifth century battle of Aylesford between the British inhabitants of the Kingdom of Kent and the new Anglo-Saxon invaders. Our earliest source for the invasion is the near contemporary account *The Ruin of Britain*, written in Latin in about 540 by the British monk Gildas who recounts how Germanic *federati* were 'let into the island like wolves into the fold, to beat back the peoples of the north' (the Picts, who were raiding down the east coast).

The Venerable Bede's *Ecclesiastical History of the English People*, written in 731, is influenced by Gildas's general account, but he also has a local Kentish source, mentioned in his 'Preface' where he says: 'My principal authority and advisor in this work has been the most reverend Abbot Albinus'. Albinus was Abbot of the Monastery of St Peter and St Paul in Canterbury (later known as St Augustine's) from 709 to 732 and it is probably in the material he gave Bede that the legendary brothers Hengist and Horsa make their first chronicle appearances. As some recent historians have doubted the existence of the brothers it is worth emphasising that Albinus was a highly respected scholar and abbot only some 250 years after the invasion and probably drawing on traditions from his monastery. Hengist turns up in the Finn episode in the epic Anglo-Saxon poem *Beowulf*, which seems to be recounting an historical event for which there is some general supporting archaeological evidence and which involves the guile, political acumen and leadership qualities we associate with Hengist's manoeuvrings in Kent. Bede tells us in chapter fifteen of his *History* that: 'Their first chieftains are said to have been the brothers Hengist and Horsa'. The brothers were probably of royal stock and from the continent, as Bede gives their descent from the god Woden (forefather of the Germanic kings) and says that Hengist founded the Anglo-Saxon dynasty and that Ethelbert, who welcomed the founder of Albinus's monastery, Augustine, was a direct descendant:

> Ethelbert was son of Irminric, son of Octa, and after his grandfather Oeric, surnamed Oisc, the kings of the Kentish folk are commonly known as Oiscings. The father of Oeric was Hengist, who first came to Britain with his son Oeric at the invitation of Vortigern.

The *Kentish Chronicle*, included in the early-ninth-century British historical compilation under the generic name of 'Nennius', gives the first account of Vortigern's marriage to Hengist's daughter and the ceding of the kingdom of Kent to the Saxons. This story is repeated by Geoffrey of Monmouth and other early chroniclers, but the favourite Kent telling of the story is in William Lambarde's *Perambulation of Kent* in 1570 under the title of 'Roxena – the first wasseling cuppe':

> [Hengist] Espying therefore, that King Vortiger was muche delighted in woman's companie... he had him to a solemn banquet, and after that he had... well plied him with pots, he let slippe before him a faire gentlewoman, his owne daughter, called Roxena, or Rowen, which being instructed before hand how to behave herself, most amiablie presented him with a goblet of wine, saying in her owne language 'Hail, noble king, wassail Lord King... with which daliance, the King was so delighted, that he not only vouchsafed to pledge her, but desired also to perform it in the right manner of her owne countrey. And therefore he answered (as he was taught unto her againe, drinc hael... Which when she had done, himself tooke the cuppe, and pledged her so hartely, that from thenceforth he could never be in rest, until he had obtained her to wife, little weighing, either how deeply he had endaungered his conscience in matching himselfe with a Heathen woman, or how greatly he had hazarded his crowne by joyning handes with so mightie a foreign nation.
>
> At the time of this marriage, Hengist (labouring by all meanes to bring in his owne countriemen) begged of the king the territories of Kent, Essex, Middlesex, and Suffolke, (then knowne by other names) pretending in worde, that he would, in consideration thereof, keep out Aurel. Ambrose (a competitor of the crowne) whose arrival King Vortiger had much feared.

The early chroniclers also refer to the wars waged in Kent by Vortigern's sons, Vortimer and Catigern against Hengist and Horsa. Bede, in the eight century, says that Horsa 'was subsequently killed in battle against the Britons, and was buried in east Kent, where a monument bearing his name still stands'; this was later tentatively identified as a cairn of flints at the village of Horsted (suggested as meaning 'Horsa's Place').

Nearly nine hundred years later the same tradition concerning Horsa is reported in Camden's *Britannia* (translated into English by Holland in 1610), which refers to traditions of the deaths of Horsa and Catigern in a battle at Aylesford and locates Catigern's burial at Kits Coty House, a prehistoric burial chamber near Bluebell Hill:

> In this battaile were slaine the generalls of both sides, Catigern the Britone, and Horsa the Saxon. Of whom the one, burned at Horsted not farre from hence, gave name to the place: and Catigern honoured with a stately and

solemne funerall is thought to have beene enterred neere unto Ailesford where under the side of a hill I saw foure huge rude, hard stones erected, two for the sides, one transversall in the midst betweene them, and the hugest of all piled and laied over them...Verily the unskilfull common people terme it at this day, of the same Catigern, Keiths or Kits Coty house.

Kits Coty House megalithic tomb was constructed several thousand years before the Battle of Aylesford, but later cultures often sought to explain such mysterious sites by connecting them to their legendary heroes or protagonists. Lambarde's *Perambulation of Kent* (1570) seems to be the first recorded connection between Catigern and Kits Coty House. The appellation 'house' still causes confusion today – some years ago when walking up to the monument we met a disappointed family who complained that 'it was not a house at all but just a heap of stones'!

Across the other side of the ancient Bluebell Hill track lies the remains of another prehistoric monument, demolished in 1690, called Little Kits Coty House. According to the historian Hercules Ayleway in 1722, Kits Coty House and Little Kits Coty House, were raised over the bodies of rival kings of Kent who died in battle with each other. Little Kits Coty in its fragmentary state is now also known as 'The Countless Stones', one of several prehistoric sites in Britain where it is said to be impossible to count the number of stones accurately. A Kentish traditional story tells of a baker who planned to count the stones by putting loaves on them. Unfortunately the loaves disappeared as soon as he took his eyes off them.

Surprisingly there are a couple of Arthurian sites in Kent, but one of these at least – Dover Castle, where there is an 'Arthur's Hall' and apparently used to be a Guinevere's Tower or Bower – is likely to be a medieval connection rather than a contemporary association. Sir Thomas Malory in his fifteenth century *Morte d'Arthur* places the first of the Arthur-Mordred battles as a sea battle at Dover, where Arthur forces a landing, but Gawain is mortally wounded. The next battle between Arthur and Mordred according to Malory is at Barham Down, with Arthur again being victorious and retreating into Canterbury.

William the Conqueror's Norman invasion gave rise to the legend of *Invicta* – the unconquered Kent; this is William Lambarde's version:

After such time as Duke William the Conqueror had overthrown King Harold in the field, at Battell in Sussex and had received the Londoners to mercy, he marched with his army towards the castle of Dover, thinking thereby to have brought in subjection this Country of Kent also. But Stigande, the Archbishop of Canterbury, and Egelsine, the Abbot of

St. Augustines, perceiving the danger, assembled the Countrymen together and laid before them the intolerable pride of the Normanes that invaded them and their own miserable condition if they should yield unto them. By which means they so enraged the common people, that they ran forthwith to weapon, and meeting at Swanscombe, elected the Archbishop and the Abbot for their Captains. This done, each man got him a green bough in his hand and beare it over his had, in such sort, as when the Duke approached, he was much amased therewith, thinking at the first that it had been some miraculous wood that moved toward him. But they, as soon as he came within hearing, cast away their boughs from them, and at the sound of a trumpet bewraied their weapons, and withall despatched towards him a messenger, which spake unto him in this manner: 'The Commons of Kent (most noble Duke) are ready to offer thee either Peace or Warr, at thy own choice and election: Peace with their faithfull Obedience, if thou wilt permit them to enjoy their ancient Liberties; Warr, and that most deadly, if thou deny it them.

We know that William compensated the townsfolk of Dover for damage to their property so presumably a deal was done with the Normans.

Monsters & Devils

Kent has had its fair share of traditional ghosts and monsters. One of the earliest sightings recorded is by a medieval monk and chronicler, Ralph of Coggeshall, who reports an incident of June 1205:

In the holy night of John the Baptist, all night thunder roared and lightning, terrific, incessantly flashed all over England. A certain strange monster was struck by lightning at Maidstone, in Kent, where, in the highest degree, the most horrible thunder reverberated. This monster had the head of an ass, the belly of a human being, and other monstrous members and limbs of animals very unlike each other. Its black corpse was scorched and so intolerable a stench came from it that hardly anyone was able to go near it.

Many counties have traditions of spectral hounds, wish-hounds or black dogs. Kent's version is 'The Great Dogg of Trottiscliffe'; the earliest reference traced by Charles Igglesden in his *Saunters in Kent* is a seventeenth-century letter with the enigmatic comment: 'July 1654, today a man was found dead on the upper road, the Great Dogg having been seen again'. He next cites an appearance to two peddlers in 1745 as they were walking on the Pilgrim's Way from Trottiscliffe towards the Medway. One of the travellers saw a 'great lean hound with prick't ears' behind them; later it suddenly appeared in front of them and savaged one of the peddlers, who was reputedly buried on the spot.

A Victorian account from Revd Edward 'H.ne' (to protect him, his full name was not given in the original document) has some similar features. He and a friend were returning from a visit to Boxley Church to Burham when:

> At a point where the road ascends... in its course, we paused to take breath, and look't back and were surprised to see some distance behind us, and standing on the way we had come, a lean grey dog with upstanding ears... I was struck by its size – it appeared as big as a calf.

As with the earlier incident the hound then suddenly appeared in front of the walkers, snarling at them and pursuing them to what the Reverend H calls the 'Druid Stone' (presumably the White Horse Stone); but on this occasion it did not make physical contact.

Igglesden also mentions the Black Dog of Shurland Hall in the Isle of Sheppey, which manifests itself in the early hours of the morning, and a long-bodied dog with a human head which haunts Skull's Gate Farm, of Cranbrook High Street. Leeds Castle was reputed in Edwardian times to be haunted by a curly-haired retriever that disappeared through walls and closed doors.

A number of Kentish proverbs mention the Devil: 'Parsley goes nine times to the Devil before it comes up' and

> Deal, Dover and Harwich,
> The devil gave his daughter in marriage;
> And, by a codicil of his well,
> He added Helveot and the Brill

The Devil decided to dispose of Canterbury, taking three sackfuls of people to the coast, but St Thomas intervened after the Sacristan of Canterbury Cathedral rang the great bell. The first two sackfuls were of the most wicked and went straight to Hell; the people in the third sack weren't so bad and founded Whitstable!

Heroes

There are a number of early traditions of King Harold surviving the Battle of Hastings and becoming a monk at Waltham Abbey, Chester, Canterbury or Dover. The Canterbury version stems from a twelfth-century Icelandic saga, *Heming Asliksson*:

The night after Harold had fallen, a peasant and his wife drove their cart to the battlefield to strip the dead. They saw a bright light shining above the great heaps of corpses and decided that there must be a holy man among them. As they were clearing away the bodies on the spot where they saw the light, a man's arm came up out of the corpses, on it a great gold ring. The peasant took hold of the arm and asked whether its owner were still alive. "I am alive", came the answer. The woman said: "I believe this is the King".

They unearthed him and took him home with them. Next day, Heming Aslaksson, a Norwegian formerly in Harold's service, came to see him. Heming offered to raise an army to win back the kingdom, but Harold said he knew that many of the English had already sworn fealty to William and he would not be the cause of their breaking their oaths. "I wish now to follow the example of King Olaf Tryggvason", he said; a hermitage should be built for him at Canterbury, so he could watch William when he went to church.

Three years later, William heard the bells ringing all over Canterbury, and asked the cause. Heming answered, "I understand that a monk has died, whose name was Harold."

"Harold who?" asked the King.

"Godwinson," answered Heming.

"Who has been seeing to him?" said the King.

"I have," responded Heming.

"If so, you are a dead man," said the King, "But let me see the body."

Heming led him to the cell where the hermit's body lay. It was naked and everyone recognised Harold. After that, William had Harold's body clothed in royal attire and buried with the greatest honour.

The *Life of Harold* (from around 1216) recounts that Harold went on pilgrimage after surviving the battle of Hastings and then lived for ten years as an anchorite in a cave near Dover, before moving to Chester.

Thomas à Becket's parents are the subjects of a legendary story known in both Kent and London in the medieval period. The story is an archetypal one of a crusader falling in love with his Muslim gaoler's daughter who sets him free and subsequently marries him. The best known version is that of the traditional ballad 'Lord Bateman', but there is a version of this still in folk singers' repertoires in Sussex and Kent called 'Lord Becket'. The essence of the tradition is that Gilbert Becket went on a crusade to the Holy Land and was captured and imprisoned by a Saracen prince whose daughter set him free on condition that when he reached England he would send for her. When he didn't keep his promise, Mahout set out in search of him, knowing only the words 'Gilbert' and 'London' (where he lived). She found him, became a Christian and married him. They were said to be buried in the graveyard of Old St Paul's and the *White Book of the City of London* (1419) records a ceremony by their graves as often forming parts of devotional visits to St Paul's by the London Corporation – Gilbert was an influential merchant. A crescent moon – a Muslim symbol – in the roof of Canterbury Cathedral above Becket's tomb is said to be a symbolic reference to the story.

Ghosts

A considerable number of reported ghostly sightings in Kent are of famous people. There are many sightings of Charles Dickens, for instance, the most famous of which is his supposed regular Christmas Eve appearance before 'the moon faced clock' (as Dickens called it in *The Seven Poor Travellers*) of The Corn Exchange in Rochester, where, on the final stroke of midnight, he slowly takes a gold watch out of his waistcoat pocket and checks the time before dematerialising.

Other Christmas Eve apparitions are the ghost of Anne Boleyn which appears on the bridge over the moat at Hever Castle, the spectre of a knight, supposed to be one of Becket's murderers, who rides up to the door of Kemsing church and dismounts and a coach at Bloor's Place, near Rainham, driven by a headless coachman, pulled by headless horses and with a headless passenger inside.

Less seasonal are the haunting of the Chequers Inn, Bickley, by the ghost of Dick Turpin, and of Hall Place in Bexley by the ghost of the Black Prince. The Cardinal's Error pub in Tonbridge was once a farmhouse on the Tonbridge Priory Estate and its modern name refers to the 'error' attributed by Shakespeare to its landowner, Cardinal Wolsey. There are several traditions of haunting, both ancient and modern, but those connected with Wolsey seem to be recent conjecture. More interesting are consistent reports over a number of years of the haunting of one of the bedrooms by a lady in a broad-brimmed hat. There is also poltergeist activity, including the falling off the wall of pictures, said to be generated by the ghost of Nellie, a servant at the farm who committed suicide. Our Tonbridge Folk Club was held in the bar of the pub for many years and on the opening night, during the singing of the first song (by one of the authors!) a picture fell off the wall; the Club is still called 'Nellie's'. All sorts of supernatural activity has been reported by those working at, living in or visiting the farm and pub; the most recent phenomenon is reported to be a phantom collie dog, to which other dogs are sensitive.

The ghost of the regicide Sir Harry Vane, executed on Tower Hill, has been seen walking on June evenings in the grounds of his house at

Fairlawne in the village of Plaxtol, carrying his head under his arm. His wife's ghost has been sighted in the same grove, wringing her hands with grief.

Restoration House, used by Dickens as Miss Haversham's residence in *Great Expectations*, is haunted by a very beautiful girl in white who leaves the property, crosses The Vines opposite and disappears. A lady in white also haunts Rochester Castle.

Bilsingham Priory, a one-time Augustinian order which had turned into a farmhouse by the nineteenth century, is sited not far from Folkestone and is the apparently the scene of numerous hauntings. In the early nineteenth century there were reports of a prior, furiously and audibly 'telling' his beads, and in addition the noise of a falling object and smashing china at night. The latter example is thought to be the last act of a woman beaten to death by her farmer husband for dropping a tray of crockery. Joseph Conrad's wife Jessie described a fascinating supernatural encounter while staying in this house:

> Suddenly I heard a terrified whimper from the dog. As I gazed at the opposite wall, which seemed to dissolve before my eyes, the room became filled with a choking dust and gritty fog, and through the haze I saw a long procession of habited monks.
>
> Slowly they passed along a hidden flight of steps, their wooden patterns sounding in ghostly rhythm as they climbed. The return of the farmer's wife with the lamp dispelled the vision or whatever it was I saw; and yet it seemed to verify it for she said: 'We can tell the time by the monks' footsteps, six o'clock every evening'. The time was exactly six o'clock.

Novelist Robert Neuman lived at 'The Pest House', Cranbrook, which was built in 1369 and used as a hospital for a short time. His novel *The Plague House Papers* describes the ghost of Theresa Benenden, daughter of a seventeenth-century owner of the house, who is said to haunt it.

Pluckley is reputed to be the most haunted village in Kent, and many of the ghosts belonging to the Deering family. During the English Civil War, Lord Deering eluded capture by the Puritans by jumping through a curved-top window and subsequently had his manor house built with windows of this type, a style frequently copied in the village. Other ghosts from the Deering family include two 'red ladies', one of whom is buried in three coffins! The ghost of a white lady has been seen on occasions at the site of the manor house. Other reported ghosts from Pluckley are a stage coach and four, a schoolteacher, a gipsy woman who sets fire to herself at the crossroads, a screaming man, a former landlord of 'The Black Horse' public house and a Colonel.

The White Horse at Chilham was formerly the vicarage of the Revd Sampson Hieran (who died in 1677), whose ghost is sometimes sighted at ten minutes past ten in the morning as 'a grey-haired old man, in black gown and gaiters, standing gazing into the fire with his hands behind his back'. Also at Chilham, a cowled monk has supposedly been seen meeting a spectral horse.

Sounds of babies crying in Reculver Churchyard in the nineteenth century led to people electing not to be buried there 'because of them spirits'. The Shipwright's Arms at Faversham has the ghost of a ship-wrecked sea captain who struggled there only to die. Lympe Castle (near the site of a Roman Saxon Shore fort) has the ghost of a Roman soldier. The very attractive and ancient Coopers' Arms in Rochester has the legend of a ghost who was a member of the Brethren of Coopers and was walled up to die for some offence to the Order and who is reported to appear once each November at night. Parts of the building date from 1199, when it was used for brewing for the nearby Priory, and the premises were licensed in 1543 just after the closure of the Priory, the name coming from the nearby cooperage.

The Ingoldsby Legends

The Revd Richard Harris Barham (1788-1845), writing under the pseudonym Thomas Ingoldsby and the author of *The Ingoldsby Legends*, was known to not only have recorded a number of Kentish legends but also to have invented some as well. Barham was born in Canterbury in 1788 into a family that claimed descent from Reginald Fitz Urse, one of the Norman knights involved in the assassination of Thomas à Becket. Barham's father, a rich hop-merchant, who weighed in at an elephantine twenty-seven stone, was a well-loved 'legend' in his own day. When he died, it was recorded that a massive crowd congregated to watch carpenters remove the entire front door of the Barham's Canterbury house in order that the undertakers could bring out the huge coffin.

Richard Barham was educated at St Paul's School, London, and Brasenose College, Oxford and took holy orders in 1813. Even his juvenile writings were distinguished by good-natured wit and a sense of fun. A religious vocation was not allowed to diminish his love of a practical joke, and as a young man he founded the Wits' Club for like-minded lovers of 'mirth'. His versions of legends in verse and prose appeared periodically in *Bentley's Miscellany* in 1837, a magazine edited by Charles Dickens, with illustrations by Teniel, Leech and Cruickshank. Barham's contributions made him famous, and were later collected in three volumes and issued as *The Ingoldsby Legends*.

Some of Barham's tales are undoubtedly the product of his own imagination, or re-workings of legends from other parts of England or European in origin; others are witty, poetic or prose re-modellings of old Kentish legends. *Nell Cook is* one such tale. Set in Canterbury in 'bluff King Harry's days' prior to the Reformation, it tells the story of a substantial and pretty young woman called Nell, who serves as cook and mistress to one of the Cathedral canons. The lecherous canon introduces a younger and prettier mistress into his house whom he pretends is his 'niece'. After six weeks, Nell can stand it no more and she poisons them both. Nell then abruptly disappears and it is rumoured that she has been buried alive under the heavy paving slabs in the 'Dark Entry', one of the gateways which leads into the cloister precinct. From this spooky spot, Nell emerges to haunt the area every Friday night. Barham claims that her story was at one time a favourite of the 'Kings' scholars' (Canterbury Cathedral schoolboys) who believed that the merest glimpse of her means that one will die within twelve months.

In the *Leech of Folkestone*, Barham sets the scene in the Romney Marsh area of Kent, jokingly spoken of locally as the fifth continent of the world, 'The World… is divided into Europe, Asia, Africa, America and Romney Marsh'. The tale (a Barham invention) concerns a local conjuror and quack doctor, Aldrovando, who conducts awesome séances on a prehistoric barrow, Aldington Knoll, by moonlight. Kentish tradition (not mentioned by Barham) has it that any investigation of the mound will bring bad luck, for the knoll contains the skeleton of a giant with a massive sword and is guarded by ghouls – the ghosts of drowned sailors. Barham mentions some local beliefs on witchcraft: in the worst of storms, Kent witches were said to sail round Dungeness Point in eggshells, and to skim shrieking on their broomsticks over the three-mile sea-dyke, Dymchurch Wall.

The Isle of Sheppey in Kent is the setting for Barham's prose story of *Grey Dolphin* which deals with legendary events surrounding a real-life knight, Sir Thomas de Shurland who was a Crusader in 1271 and who was knighted at the siege of Caerlaverock. His tomb and effigy are in the south aisle of Minster church. A stone horse's head is carved beside the warrior's right leg while his sword and spear lie to the left of the knight. A former local name for the church was 'Horse Church' and an unusual 'horse-vane' is set on the tower. 'Grey Dolphin' was the name of Sir Thomas's charger which had accompanied him on the Crusades.

Barham's frolicsome story takes liberties with the local tradition which is that the Lord of Shurland while riding past the churchyard of the Minster became concerned that a drowned seaman was being interred without prayers being said over the grave. In Barham's story, a friar is summoned but refuses the Lord's reasonable request to perform a short service whereupon Sir Thomas loses his temper, stabs the friar and throws him into the open grave. In order to escape ecclesiastical justice, Sir Thomas flees to the coast and, still on horseback, swims out to the king's ship, moored off the Isle of Sheppey, a daunting distance of two miles. Here the knight obtains the king's pardon but on his return to Sheppey a 'cunning woman' forecasts his death – with Grey Dolphin as the cause. To avert the tragedy, Sir Thomas kills his faithful steed. A year later, while riding over the sands where he had killed Grey Dolphin, his horse stumbles over the old charger's bones, whereupon Sir Thomas is thrown headlong and killed.

The Brothers of Birchington is Barham's reworking of an old legend which explains why Reculver church has twin towers. The Kent legend, known as the 'Twin Sisters' tells how two nuns, the Abbess of Davington and her sister, were making a pilgrimage by sea to the chapel of Our Lady of Broadstairs when they were caught in a storm and wrecked off the Kent coast at Reculver. The Abbess, in gratitude for her own life and as a memorial to her drowned sister, paid for the two towers to be built as a beacon for mariners. Barham alters the story so that he can be both funny and disrespectful. His two protagonists are twin brothers who have become monks in an enclosed religious foundation; they are Robert and Richard, the 'Brothers of Birchington'. Richard, who is the Prior of the religious order, is a pious and exemplary monk. However, his twin brother Robert is a wordly and fleshly minded man despite his vows. The Devil determines to claim his own and sends his bailiff to lead Robert to hell where he undoubtedly belongs. Unable to distinguish which twin is which, the diabolical servant 'grabb'd Dick when he *should* have nabb'd Bob' and his evil Dark Master apologetically restores the saintly Richard to the world of men. It is the brothers (not the sisters) who, according to Barham, caused the towers to be built:

> On the verge of the land,
> To warn mariners off from the Columbine sand,
> And many a poor man have Robert and Dick
> By their vow caused to 'scape, like themselves, from Old Nick.

9

ANTISOCIAL CUSTOMS

The public sales of wives with halters round their necks at market places or in pubs is well-attested in most counties in the eighteenth and nineteenth centuries and Thomas Hardy's use of the custom in his novel *The Mayor of Casterbridge* has drawn widespread attention to it. E.P. Thompson, in his book *Customs in Common*, concludes that the custom, far from intending to belittle women, was actually a kind of common-law method of achieving divorce, with the consent of all parties symbolised ritually and leading to a new union, operating at the lower end of society where legal and religious divorce were impossible.

The example from Kent in 1828 which he cites (one of ten he has traced) seems to bear this out. The three people concerned, a Mr and Mrs Skinner and Mrs Skinner's new lover, Mr Savage, shared a parish cottage in Speldhurst. The overseers of the poor threatened them with eviction for immoral behaviour, and they decided to remedy the situation by a public transfer of the woman from one to the other at the 'George and Dragon' public house which still exists at Tonbridge. A charge of a misdemeanour was brought to the West Kent Quarter Sessions and the publican gave evidence as follows:

> Skinner came first, and asked for a pot of beer; he sat in the kitchen; his wife then came in, and shortly after Savage entered; they all drank together, and

in a little time Savage went out; he soon returned, and Skinner then said to him, "Will you buy my wife?" He replied, "What will you have for her?" Skinner said, "A shilling and a pot of beer." Savage then tendered him half a crown, and Skinner delivered his wife to him; they drank together, and then went away; there were about four persons present; before they went, the woman took a handkerchief from her pocket-hole, which appeared to have been round her waist, and Skinner taking it, said, "I've now nothing more to do with you, and you may go with Savage."

The Chairman of the Bench commented that the crime would have been greater if committed in open market; he felt the crime had been committed 'in a state of ignorance' (the parties presumably thought the new contract was legally and morally binding), and therefore gave what he thought was a lenient punishment of one month's imprisonment each. Two other points are worth making: Skinner was living in the workhouse at the time of the trial, so the defendants had ceased to be a 'ménage a trois' and presumably thought this would silence the criticism, and Mrs Skinner was definitely in favour of the transaction (rather than feeling herself demeaned by it) as she commented at the trial that 'My husband did not go on to my wishes, and that was the reason I wished to part'.

Seven years earlier there had been another example of wife-selling in Tonbridge, spotted by the *Journal of the Kent Family History Society* and contributed to the Tonbridge Civic Society Newsletter:

13th April 1821
WIFE SOLD AT MARKET
On Tuesday, a man having the appearance of a horse jockey sold his wife at Tunbridge market for one shilling and sixpence and a pot of beer. She was a very pretty young woman and declared her husband was such a good-for-nothing rascal that she could not live with him – an assertion for the truth of which she deserves full credit.

George Frampton has unearthed a further seven cases of wife selling in Kent from local newspapers such as the *Maidstone Journal* and the *Kentish Gazette* dating to the first half of the nineteenth century, including one from his own village of Marden; these are listed in an article in volume twenty-two of the excellent local folklore magazine *Bygone Kent*. The accounts appear to indicate that husbands were openly selling their wives in the busy cattle markets held at Canterbury, Maidstone, Hythe and Cranbrook. In one case the husband having mistaken market day, elected to sell his wife in a public tavern, and another transaction was also made in a pub. In five of these instances the purchase seems to have been previously agreed – the purchaser accompanied the married couple to the place of sale. So this invaluable further evidence broadly bears out E.P. Thompson's theory. The most dramatic of the cases is from the *Maidstone Journal* dated June 1847:

> On Thursday last, the following iniquitous scene was witnessed in Maidstone Market. A man (formerly of Marden) named William Payne, sold his wife and two children to a person named James Laddams, of Marden, for ten shillings. The woman was led in to the market with a halter round her neck, and thus exposed for sale, and after the purchase had been completed, the man and woman returned to an adjacent Inn and indulged themselves with a hearty dinner. Immediately after this nefarious transfer had been concluded, the wife coolly addressed her husband, "Well, George, after this, I hope you will not molest me any more, nor attempt to come near me", to which her husband replied, "No, not as long as I live". On returning to Marden, by which time all parties were far from sober, an altercation took place about the husband's furniture, which his successor declared was included in the bargain. A fight ensued, which ended in Payne being stabbed in the face with a knife, though not seriously. The mother of the woman was sold at Cranbrook, under similar circumstances, some years ago.

Kentish couples living together not as man and wife were wryly referred to as 'married at Finglesham Church', the point being that the small village had no church. At Brookland church on Romney Marsh, marriage was said to be so rare that when a couple asked to be married there the steeple jumped off the church roof in surprise – an interesting story devised to explain the adjacent bell tower at Brookland.

Poaching

Some antisocial customs existed for economic reasons. Smuggling (see chapter three) could be considered antisocial, but it depends on your perspective, as many communities relied on it for survival and many individuals benefited financially. Smugglers, although defrauding the exchequer in the manner of import duties, did purchase their goods rather than steal them. The moral position of poaching was also ambiguous. Poachers were stealing animals and birds from landowners, but could claim that wild animals belonged to everyone before the Norman estates and the later enclosures of commons (themselves of doubtful legality) removed a source of food from the common people:

> A buck, a doe, believe me so, a pheasant or a hare,
> Was set on earth for everyone quite equal for to share
>
> *The Rufford Park Poachers*

As with smugglers, poachers could be regarded as heroes by the ordinary people, particularly if they refused to turn Queen's evidence. Take the song well known in Kent and Sussex, 'Willie Taylor'; this version was collected from the singing of Ken Thompson, formerly of Little Betsoms Farm, north of Westerham, as recently as the late 1980s:

> *Now all you good people, come listen awhile.*
> *I'll sing you a ditty will cause you to smile.*
> *Concerning some keepers and poachers also,*
> *Who fought in those covies some winters ago.*
>
> *Now when we go in boys, good luck to us all,*
> *Our guns will go off and the pheasants will fall.*
> *In less than ten minutes Twelve keepers are spied,*
> *Saying, "Come you bold poachers, how dare you come night."*
>
> *Now said one to the other, "Well what shall we do?"*
> *Said one to the other, "We all should stand true".*
> *They all did agree for to be all as one,*
> *And to fight the bold keepers till the battle was won.*
>
> *Now there was one Willie Taylor who did not run away,*
> *For five of those keepers all on him did play,*
> *Young William being tired, he lay down to rest.*
> *Young William was taken, though he was the best.*
>
> *Now the judges and jury to him they did say,*
> *"If you will confess, your sweet life we will save."*
> *"O no", said young Taylor, "That won't do at all.*
> *For now that you've got me, I'll die for them all."*
>
> *Now there's none like young Taylor, that's ever been yet.*
> *There's none like young Taylor you people can bet.*
> *There's none like young Taylor you people all know,*
> *Who fought in those covies some winters ago.*

The *Tonbridge Free Press* records the fining of a poacher from the nearby village of Capel as recently as January 1942:

POACHER FINED

John C___ of 6 Colts Hill Cottages, Capel, was summoned at Tonbridge Police Court on Tuesday last week by Walter T___ of W___ Farm, Capel, for trespassing on his property in search of conies.

Mr T___, in evidence said while out with his gun on his estate, he found defendant over a rabbit hole. When ordered off, defendant refused to go until he had retrieved his ferret. Witness said he would take a summons out against the defendant, and left him near the rabbit hole.

Corroborative evidence was given by an estate employee.

Defendant, who did not appear in court, wrote pleading guilty and said he thought he was doing good by helping to exterminate rabbits, which were a nuisance in that part of the country. He added that he wanted a meal for his wife and children.

Defendant, described as a married man with six children, was fined 5s.

This incident occurred in wartime when meat supplies were lower than usual; the savage game laws of the late eighteenth and nineteenth centuries (from when the *Willie Taylor* song presumably dates) had long been repressed by then, but the violent poacher gangs who fought with gamekeepers, sometimes killing or maiming them to avoid arrest in a reflection perhaps of the smuggling gangs, had also long disappeared.

Highwaymen & Footpads

Highway robbery, though, benefited no-one except the perpetrator, and Kent had its fair share of 'Gentlemen of the Road'. Geoffrey Chaucer, MP for Greenwich, was robbed on the highway on several occasions at the end of the fourteenth century and Shakespeare is drawing on Gads Hill as a notorious area for highway robbery in his play *Henry the Fourth: Part II*. The *Maidstone Journal* for 23 January 1787 mentions the trial of two highwaymen charged with committing robberies in the Blackheath area:

On Monday two highwaymen who committed many robberies on Blackheath and the Kentish roads during the course of last-week, were examined at the public office in Bow-Street. Several gentlemen attended who have recently been robbed, when sufficient proof of their guilt appearing, they were ordered for examination before Sir S. Wright and Mr Justice Addington on Friday last, concerning the robbery of Alderman Curtis, and another gentleman - No other evidence appearing to incriminate them, Manning was discharged; but without of sensible, feeling and furious admonition from Sir Sampson Wright, relative to his future conduct. - Wentworth was committed to Newgate for trial, at our next assizes. - It is said he is of good family, and was bred a surgeon, since which he has served as an officer in one of the provincial Corps in Ireland. - He appeared very much affected with his unhappy situation; into which he has undoubtedly been drawn by a deliberately designing villain, who has thus far escaped the hands of justice.

Robert Goodsall in his *A Second Kentish Patchwork* quotes several examples in *The Canterbury Press* of 1770 for attacks in the Shooter's Hill area:

April 21, 1770
Friday morning last a Lady was stopped in a post-chaise near Shooters-hill by two highwaymen armed, with frightful vizors on their faces. They took all she had, amounting to near thirty pounds, and then rode away. The Lady was so terrified at their appearance that she fell into fits and remains very ill at present.

April 21, 1770
On Saturday last, about ten in the evening, two gentlemen in a post-chaise, coming over Blackheath, were stopped by a single man on foot dressed in a carter's frock. One of the gentlemen, a military officer, told the fellow, in a peremptory manner, that he would not be robbed, and desired him to desist; but the villain presented a pistol, and threatening violence, the gentleman shot him dead on the spot... The same gentlemen had not rode above three miles farther on their way to London, when they were attacked again by a highwayman well mounted, near the Red-house. The gentleman who killed the footpad shot directly at the highwayman through the blind of the chaise, and is supposed to have wounded him'.

June 19, 1770
On Saturday two gentlemen coming from London in a post-chaise, were stopt [sic] near the second mile-stone by a highwayman, who putting a pistol into the chaise, demanded their money. One of the gentlemen gave him six or seven guineas, the other about ten shillings and his watch, assuring him that was all the cash they had about them; on which the highwayman very genteelly made each of them a present of a guinea, and rode off wishing them a good journey.

Black Robin, the Ghostly Highwayman

There are traditions that refer to a supernatural highwayman, Black Robin, at the pub of the same name in Kingston. This pub faces Black Robin Lane, down which the ghost is said to ride; he is said to have been hanged on a gallows specially erected at nearby Barham Crossroads. The pub was relicensed for 8s in 1740, proving its existence prior to that date. However, 'Black Robin' was also a nickname frequently used to refer to a smuggler, and the notorious Aldington Gang frequently used the pub.

Skimmity Riding & Rough Music

Readers familiar with Hardy's *The Mayor of Casterbridge* will know about the West Country skimmity riding tradition in which those causing moral outrage in a community were paraded on horseback, either in person or effigy, to the accompaniment of rough music, and ridiculed and manhandled. There is an early Kent example of this same custom cited in *The Weald of Kent* which refers to the actions of the Canterbury mob against Archbishop Winchelsea in the very early fourteenth century:

> He appears... To have highly incensed the inhabitants of Canterbury, and they rose in a tumultuous manner, attacked his palace and servants, and pillaged his goods. They also mounted his Dean on the back of a horse, with his face towards the tail, which they compelled him to hold as a bridle, and thus proceeded to Selling with songs and dances, ending by casting the Dean into the mire.

10

A QUESTION OF CHARITY

Charitable bequests in pre-Reformation days were ways in which donors could acquire spiritual merit on and after their deaths, thus being able to mitigate the longs spells in Purgatory which the Roman Catholic religion believed intervened between death and elevation to heaven. The practice did continue throughout the sixteenth century, and many Kent churches have display boards giving details of charitable bequests, some of which continue, but there was a marked decline in the seventeenth century, when Puritan rectors, such as those at Biddenden (see below) were opposed to the continuance of practices which they felt adhered to outmoded 'Roman' beliefs. The pious nineteenth century led to a new spate of charitable foundations and bequests and the more scrupulous administration of existing ones; some practices which the Victorians felt to be unseemly in a religious context such as the distribution of beer in church, or indeed of beer at all, were revised; thus each age modifies custom according to its own beliefs and prejudices. As well as the endowed bequests, there were a number of less formal, yearly handouts to the poor, unendowed, but usually with a traditional benefactor, family, or group of benefactors. The most appropriate seasons of the church calendar for such distributions, formal and informal, were Easter (with its associations with 'maunds' and Christ's instructions to look after the poor) and Advent, particularly St Thomas's Day, where money or food could be given towards the celebration of Christmas.

The Biddenden Dole

The most famous and interesting charitable bequest in Kent is from the wool town of Biddenden, and was formerly enacted on Easter Sunday, but nowadays on Easter Monday. The bequest is attributed to Elisa and Mary Chulkhurst, legendary Siamese twins said to have been born in 1100 and to have died in 1134. The endowment of the charity originally took the form of rents from twenty acres of land and a smallholding known as 'the Bread and Cheese Lands'; produce from these lands may also have been used or sold for the purposes of the charity. In the twentieth century the land was sold for housing development (Chulkhurst Avenue etc.) and the money invested to maintain the charity, aided by rents from the Old Workhouse and a small plot of land. Part of 'the Bread and Cheese Lands' have been turned into a children's playground. The Biddenden Dole is recorded in 1646 and 1656, when the Puritan minister of the church, William Horner, tried unsuccessfully to claim the Bread and Cheese Lands as part of the Church glebe lands. The Court of the Exchequer gave judgement in 1656 that the lands which had been bequeathed belonged to the parish, rather than to the church.

The date, location and form of the charity have all changed over the centuries. The early records show that cheese, bread and beer was given to widows of the parish in the church on Easter Sunday. In 1682 the Revd Giles Hinton complained to Archbishop Sancroft that the custom: 'even to this time is with much disorder and indecency observed and needs a regulation by His Grace's Authority'. The distribution of beer and food was accordingly moved from inside the church to the church porch. During the Victorian period the venue was changed to the workhouse, the date from Easter Sunday to Easter Monday and the beverage from beer to a packet of tea. There is a record in 1872 of 538 loaves being distributed.

In 1907 the Biddenden Dole was consolidated with three other local charities. Today all senior citizens and widows of the parish can receive the dole in person or by proxy between 10 and 11 a.m. on Easter Monday at the workhouse (known as 'the White House') at the west end of the village on the Sissinghurst Road. The same beneficiaries receive money at Christmas as well. Visiting tourists are given a hard inedible biscuit made from flour and water, with a traditional pattern stamped on it of two women whose bodies seem to be joined. Over their heads are their names and the skirt of one figure has 'in 1100' inscribed on it and the other the number '34'. Edward Hasted, the distinguished Kent historian, stated in 1792 that the figures had only appeared on the biscuits some fifty years earlier and were supposed to represent the widows who claimed the dole, rather than the Chulkhurst sisters. In Hasted's day the biscuits were apparently without name or date. Hasted claimed that the dole was more recent than had been supposed by the legend and that the donors were two maiden ladies of the name Preston; these ladies were not Siamese twins and the Siamese tradition may have originated from the depiction on the biscuit of two ladies apparently conjoined.

The earliest reference to the Chulkhurst sisters appears to be a locally-printed eighteenth-century broadside for 'the edification of visitors' to the custom and given with the Biddenden biscuits. A copy was sent to William Hone who published it in his *Every Day Book*:

> In the year 1100, at Biddenden, in Kent, were born Elizabeth and Mary Chulkhurst, Joined together by the Hips and Shoulders, and who lived in that state, Thirty-Four Years!! At the expiration of which time one of them was taken ill and after a short period died; the surviving one was advised to be separated from the corpse which she absolutely refused by saying these words, 'as we came together, we will also go together,' and about six hours after her sister's decease, she was taken ill and died also. A stone near the Rector's Pew marked with a diagonal line is shown as the place of their interment. It is further stated that by their will they bequeathed to the Churchwardens of the Parish of Biddenden.

A poem on the subject discovered in the old charity documents sounds nineteenth century, showing influence from John Keats' famous 1820 poem *The Eve of St Agnes*:

> The moon on the east oriel shone
> Through slender shafts of shapely stone
> The silver light so pale and faint,
> Shewed the twin sisters and many a saint
> Whose images on the glass were dyed:
> Mysterious maidens side by side
> The moonbeams kissed the holy pane
> And threw on the pavement a mystic stain.

Other Charities

More is known of the origins of a nearby Cranbrook bequest, that of Thomas Taylor of Cranbrook, who bequeathed about seven acres of woodland (since called 'Poors Wood') in 1569 for the use of the poor. Timber from Poors

Wood was used to build the workhouse from where the Biddenden Dole is now distributed. Taylor's bequest was subsequently administered alongside the Chulkhurst Charity by the Parish and is described as having 'brought in a good return in timber sales from time to time'.

The Chittended Charity at Plaxtol is documented in 1778:

> The gift of Silas Chittended to the poor of Plaxtol borough is 10 loaves of good wheaten bread, of the value of 10d each to ten poor families on the first Sunday in November. Twenty other such loaves to the poor families of the said borough on the 6th day of January following, and 10 other such loaves to the poor if the said borough on the first Sunday in March... The above gift is the interest of £70 three per cent. Consuls.

There were also many charitable bequests for pilgrim hospices and for almshouses for the poor and elderly in the cities and towns of Kent, many of which are still being administered. Eastbridge Hospital, in St Peter's Street Canterbury, began life as a hospice for pilgrims visiting Becket's Shrine and the first Master was a relative of Becket's. After the Reformation, the accommodation became almshouses, which it remains today, but the Crypt where the pilgrims slept, their Refectory and their Chapel with its splendid roof are open to the public.

St John's Hospital Canterbury and St Nicholas's Hospital in nearby Harbledown are a twin foundation originated by Archbishop Lanfranc in the late eleventh century. St John's was founded to care for the elderly and St Nicholas's to care for lepers. St Nicholas's was ideally placed for lepers, being outside the City, on healthy high ground and with a curative well; in the twelfth century it is estimated there were over 100 lepers, male and female, living at the Hospital of the Wood of Blean, as it was then called. The founder directed that the lepers should be looked after by a chaplain and 'skilful, patient and kindly watchers'; the male uniform was a russet gown and hood and scapular and the female uniform a mantle and double veil; both men and women wore high ox-hide boots fastened with leather.

From the fourteenth century, with the great decline in leprosy, St Nicholas's Hospital gradually began to turn into almshouses. After the Reformation, Archbishop Parker issued statutes in 1565 directing that all places should be filled by the Archbishop, and that ten non-resident brothers and sisters were to be appointed on pensions. The old people were to chose a prior and prioress from amongst them and the prior was to oversee the property of the hospital, especially the woodlands, which were to be used to gather wood for fuel; he also was to ensure that the well was sufficiently fenced and 'kept from cattell' and to gather rents, place the money in a chest with three locks and keys (almost certainly the same chest that is still in the church) and to deliver annual accounts. The prioress kept the key to the frater house (where the money was kept). Every brother and sister at both St Nicholas's and St John's had to pay a 'reparation noble' on admission towards the repair of the church and houses and was required to attend church twice a day for public prayer, on pain of half a day in the stocks.

Sandwich had three medieval hospitals. St Bartholomew's was founded in 1190, though tradition links its founding with booty seized from the defeated fleet of Eustace the Monk at the battle of Sandwich Bay, 1217. In Tudor times it had a Patronal Feast which provided oranges for the Mayor and since 1835 has been governed by a Board of Trustees, who also adminster St Thomas's and St John's (amalgamated in the 1820s). St Bartholomew's was renovated in 1878 and provides sixteen houses for retired Sandwich people. There was formerly a dole tradition of bread, cheese and beer for children, but this has been replaced by the Bartholomew Bun Race, which consists of a run round St Bartholomew's Chapel for a bun apiece on St Bartholomew's Day (24 August). Adults visiting this custom are given a St Bartholomew Biscuit bearing the design of the hospital seal.

The Watts Charity

The well-known Richard Watts Charity at Rochester was used by Charles Dickens for one of his Christmas stories, *The Seven Poor Travellers*. Dickens visited the Watts Charity in May 1854, signing the visitor's book, and using it as a setting for a group of stories by the six travellers (written by various authors including Wilkie Collins) plus himself as narrator, and published in the December 1854 edition of his magazine *Household Words*:

> Strictly speaking, there were only six Poor Travellers; but, being a Traveller myself, though an idle one, and being as poor as I hope to be, I brought the number up to seven. This word of explanation is due at once, for what says the inscription over the quaint old door?
>
> RICHARD WATTS, Esq.
> By his Will, dated 22 Aug. 1579,
> Founded this Charity
> For Six poor Travellers,

Who not being ROGUES, or PROCTORS,
May receive gratis for one Night,
Lodging, Entertainment,
And Four-pence each.

It was in the ancient little city of Rochester in Kent, of all the good days in the year upon a Christmas Eve, that I stood reading this inscription over the quaint old door in question. I had been wandering about the neighbouring Cathedral, and had seen the tomb of Richard Watts, with the effigy of worthy Master Richard starting out of it like a ship's figure-head; and I had felt that I could do no less... than inquire the way to Watts's Charity...

I found it to be a clean white house, of a staid and venerable air, with... an arched door, choice little long low lattice-windows, and a roof of three gables. The silent High Street of Rochester is full of gables, with old beams and timbers carved into strange faces. It is oddly garnished with a queer old clock that projects over the pavement out of a grave red brick building, as if Time carried on business there, and hung out his sign.

This clock is the one associated with the ghostly appearance of Dickens on Christmas Eve (see chapter eight).

Under the terms of Richard Watts' will, 'six several rooms with chimneys' were to be added to 'the almshouse already erected and standing beside the Market-Crosse... to provide for 'six poore Travellers or Wayfareing men' who were to 'lodge for no longer than one night unless sickness be the further cause'. The lodgers were also to be given 4d – this was increased to 1s in 1934. Candidates were selected from those who applied and those chosen each received a warrant admitting them. Pauper children were also housed at the almshouses so that they could learn a trade or occupation.

Records in the nineteenth century show an average supper as being half a pound of meat, a pound of bread, and a pint of coffee in the evening and another in the morning. The last traveller was admitted on 20 July 1940. However, in 1858 further 'Watts Almshouses' had been built in Maidstone Road, Rochester, to house ten men and ten women; five of the women were to provide a nursing service for the occupants of the almshouses and also for the poor of Rochester. In 1977 eleven bungalows were added and the almshouses now cater for forty residents and three members of staff. The Almshouse Charities in Rochester were further increased by the inclusion of Sir John Hayward's Almshouses and St Catherine's Hospital and by the conversion of Reeves House in Watts Avenue into seven flats for married couples. The Richard Watts Charity is still playing an active role in local society by providing almshouse accommodation, paying grants and providing a home help service to non-residents; the early interest in children has been continued by educational grants.

Goodening

The St Thomas's Day (21 December) charities reflect active, but traditionally expected, begging, particularly on the part of widows; it is variously known in Kent as 'gooding', 'goodening', 'mumping' and 'dawdlin'. This Advent custom is conveniently placed for Christmas largesse, but the traditional Kentish explanation for the date is that St Thomas had to pay for doubting the resurrection of Christ and the custom commemorates this. In reality, in the Roman Catholic church, the dating of significant or festive events was often by using saints days. By the early nineteenth century the survival of gooding was strongest in the villages around Maidstone. William Hone's *Every Day Book* of 1825 comments on the survival of the custom at Loose, Linton and Barming:

> At Loose, Mr T. Charlton gives the poor of the parish certain quantities of wheat, apportioned to their families, in addition to which, his daughters give the widows a new flannel petticoat each, who at the same time, go to the other respectable inhabitants of the place to solicit the usual donatory, and it is not an uncommon thing for a family to get in this way six or seven shillings... the custom is also prevalent at Linton an adjoining parish; and I am also informed that Lord Cornwallis, who resides there, intends giving to the resident poor something very considerable. At Barming, C. Whittaker, Esq is provided with one hundred loaves to distribute to the resident poor on this day, which to my knowledge is annual on his part; they likewise go to other respectable inhabitants, who also give their alms in the way they think best.

Alfred Moore, in an article in the *Kentish Gazette* on the subject of 'Goodenin' in April 1895, defines the custom as 'the going round just before Christmas of poor people to the residences of more wealthy neighbours to solicit small gifts of money (occasionally of meal or floor also) the request being generally put in the formula of 'Please remember the goodenin' and the doles being goodenin gifts'.

Moore was sent very useful information by 'an old gentleman at Willesbrough' who was a resident and eyewitness of the custom at Leeds in 1845, whence it continued until about 1865. Moore describes the activity at Leeds 1845 from his informant's notes:

The goopeners (who were either widows or poor women with large families) met at a gate opposite the Ten Bells Inn at ten o'clock on the morning of St Thomas's Day. An old widow who was known as Granny Hicks was chosen 'Queen of the Goodeners', after which election they started on their 'dawdling' as it was then called. The party was under the entire control of its queen, calling only at such houses as she thought proper, the first being to Burgess Hall where Granny made a deep curtsey to Farmer Hodsell with a 'Please remember the goodeners' and was rewarded with a coin of the realm. Crossing the fields and calling at most of the houses, they reached Fulling Mill Farm where Mr Betts gave old Granny half-a-crown and a peck of wheat which was his regular custom. Crossing more fields, the party came out into the Maidstone and Ashford Road and on into the parish of Broomfield to Leeds Castle, where all the goodeners standing together curtsied to the squire, wished him a Merry Christmas and were presented with five shillings, after which they gradually worked their way by another route back to the place from whence they had started, where they arrived at about three o'clock in the afternoon after a perambulation of some six miles or more. The money which had been collected was here shared out, but I regret to say that it only amounted to eight pence for each member of the expedition in which about thirty goodeners took part.

Christmas Bread Dole at Cobham

A board in the nave of St Mary Magdalene Church in Cobham (see photo) records a Christmas Charity bequeathed by the Hayes family of Owletts, a substantial property in the village. William Hayes bequeathed through his will of 1678 for the 'Poor of this Parish for ever. TWENTY SHILLINGS (issuing out of his Lands) to be laid out in Bread on Christmas Eve annually.'

In 1789 Richard Hayes bequeathed 'to the Poor of this Parish for the Timebeing (being Householders therein) and not receiving Relief. EIGHTY POUNDS.' Richard's bequest was administered by trustees from investments and it is interesting to note that he wisely stipulated 'for the Timebeing' instead of 'for ever'!

11

THE SONGS OF THE PEOPLE

England's magnificent heritage of traditional songs and tunes is internationally acclaimed, but underrated by the academic and educational establishments and most of the general public in the south east, although some enlightened local authorities are providing financial and publicity support. The Broadstairs Folk Festival each August provides an enjoyable and well-publicised showpiece for Kentish singers, musicians and folk dancers and there are several excellent folk clubs and informal music and songs sessions in Kent, maintained by a determined body of enthusiasts and a network of fine performers deserving of wider public and tourist attendance.

Periodically there have been revivals of interest in English folk song, notably in the twenty years before the First World War, a crucial period when the rural working class was both being displaced and losing interest in its own traditional heritage. This 'first revival' was spearheaded by Cecil Sharp, a music teacher and writer who discovered the survival of a rich vein of traditional song and dance by accident in middle age and then became an assiduous collector of songs and morris dances. Much of his song collecting was in the west of England, but he paid a few visits to Kent just before the First World War.

Perhaps the most fruitful of Sharp's visits was to Joseph Beale, a poulterer in his seventies at Spothouse Farm in the village of Warehorne on the edge of the Romney Marsh. His haul on 23 September 1908 included a fine Kent version of the Easter and Christmas carol 'The Moon Shines Bright' with a distinctive tune and an unusual 'leek' metaphor:

The Moon shines bright, the stars give light
A little before it was day,
The Lord our God he calls on us
And bids us to wake and pray.

...In yonder garden green doth grow,
As green as any leek,
Our Lord our God he waters us
With his heavenly dew so sweet.

The song, with a slightly different tune, was a favourite also with mummers and carol singers in Sussex and there is a version in Sandys' *Christmas Carols* (1833).

Sharp collected two other carols from Joseph Beale, 'Sons of Levi' and the beautiful 'The Bold Fisherman', an allegorical song based on the Christian concept of Christ as a fisher of men, full of symbolism, humanistic compassion and fine poetry, also found extensively in neighbouring Sussex:

As I walked out one May morning
Down by the riverside
There I beheld a bold fisherman
Come a-rolling down the tide.
Come a-rolling down the tide,
There I beheld a bold fisherman
Come a-rolling down the tide.

Sharp also collected from Joseph Beale a version of 'The Outlandish Knight' called 'The Baffled Knight' and two other well-known folksongs, 'Cold Blow and Rainy Night' and 'The Keys of Heaven', a courtship challenge song better known in Kent as 'The Keys of Canterbury':

O Madam I will buy you a fine silken gown
And twenty yards of lace for to draggle on the ground,
If you will walk with me, with me,
If you will walk with me.

Sharp collected 'The Barley Mow' from George Benstead in 1908 at nearby Ham Street and 'The Thresherman and the Squire' from Clarke Lonkhurst.

Charles Barling of Ruckinge sang 'Lord Thomas and Fair Eleanor' and part of another version of 'The Bold Fisherman' for Sharp. In a visit to Sittingbourne in 1911, Cecil Sharp collected the carols 'The Seven Joys of Mary', 'As I Sat on A Sunny Bank' (see chapter two) and another version of 'The Moon Shines Bright' from Mrs Alice Harding.

Vaughan Williams collected a number of well-known songs at Gravesend from Mr and Mrs Truell, including 'John Reilly', 'The Pedlar Bold and Robin Hood', 'The Foggy Dew', 'Cupid's Garden' and 'Spencer the Rover'. Another well-known collector, Anne Gilchrist, collected 'Green Bushes', 'Babes in the Wood' and 'The Banks of the Sweet Primroses' from Mrs Jenner of Ashurst on the Kent-Sussex border – Mrs Jenner had learnt songs from her mother who was from Penshurst. 'Death and the Lady' – an interesting ballad with an Elizabethan flavour of personification and allegory was collected at Maidstone from the singing of Mr Baker and published in Vaughan Williams' and Bert Lloyd's *The Penguin Book of English Folk Song*:

> *My name is Death, cannot you see?*
> *Lords, dukes, and ladies bow down to me,*
> *And you are one of those branches three,*
> *And you fair maid, and you fair maid,*
> *And you fair maid must come with me.*

A substantial number of songs with Kentish connections are printed (without tunes) in volume two of *A Kentish Garland* (1882). By far the most interesting is a fine version of 'General Wolfe', an eighteenth-century soldier hero from Westerham, who offered his resignation from the army in protest at the killing of wounded Jacobites at Culloden and then died an heroic death scaling the Heights of Abraham at Quebec. The editor of the *Garland* says that 'Mrs A.J. Woodhouse, of Ide-Hill Vicarage, kindly procured [the song] from an old man who used to sing it at the residence of her family, the Oxendens of Eastwell Rectory, on every New Year's Day, and who wrote it out at her request'. The song (and tune fortunately) are quite well known, having been found extensively in recent East Anglian tradition; this Kent version is slightly corrupt (especially the extraordinary first line):

> *Come, all you lads of cordial balls,*
> *And never seem daunted wherever you go;*
> *To fight the French is our delight,*
> *Like lads of honour, like lads of honour,*
> *With courage stout and bold.*

General Wolf unto his men did say,
"My lads, be steady and stand by me."
Each what a sight it is to behold,
Seventeen thousand, seventeen thousand
Lay bleeding on the ground.

They was upon mountains high
And we down on valleys low.
He gave command on the field he did lay;
"Lads, fight on so boldly, fight on so boldly,
Gain the victory and die."

The very first they gave to us
It wounded our general in his right breast,
"Well done, my lads" General Wolf did say,
"Fight on so boldly, fight on so boldly,
Gain the victory and die."

The very first we gave to them
We made the French dogs for to run.
"Well done, my lads', General Wolf did say,
"Fight on so boldly, fight on so boldly,
While I have life I got command."

It is kernel Captain unto his men did say,
"Oh, take me by my lily white hand
While the blood out of my tender breast do fly
Just like a fountain, just like a fountain,
Just like a fountain, so do not greve for me.

Here is my treasure all in bright gold,
Take it and part it, for my blood runs cold;
Share it amongst you," General Wolf did say,
"You are welcome to it, you are welcome to it,
Now you have gained the victory.

When to old England you do return,
You may tell my friends I am dead and gone;
You may tell my tender old Mother dear
Not to weep for me, not to weep for me,
For she will never see me more."

The Kentish Garland includes many eighteenth-century broadside ballads from collections now in the British Library which although printed outside Kent, feature Greenwich and Kent ports, usually romantically linking sailors to young ladies. A typical example is 'The Jolly Sailor and the Lady of Greenwich':

A Lady Born of birth and fame,
To Greenwich Town for pleasure came,
Where she a sailor did behold,
Both tall and trim, of courage bold.

Other titles include 'Ned Flint and Kate of Dover', 'The Young Sailor from Dover', 'Fair Betsy of Deptford', 'Peggy of Deal', 'The Greenwich Lovers' Garland', 'Greenwich Moorings', 'Jack of Greenwich' and 'The Greenwich Pensioner's Garland'.

The collection contains an interesting hunting song, 'The Lullingstone Hunt' taken from Charles Armiger's *Sportsman's Vocal Cabinet* (1830) which deliberately invokes a number of famous northern Kent sites:

On the third of September, I think thereabout,
From the Lullingstone kennel the hounds were led out;
The harvest was over, the morning as bright
As ever succeeded the darkness of night:
Dick Carter, the huntsman, a rider as bold
As e'er cross'd a saddle in heat or in cold.

Stout Reynold unkennele'd; we gave him some law,
When he took through the stubbles, to Allington-ha,
Then dash'd through the Medway, just under the mill,
And fled like a swallow the steeps of Bell-hill:
Where in Kit's Coity-house he determin'd to wait
(The old Kentish tomb that tells Catigern's fate)...

The fox is pursued through Horsted, Marden, Blue Bell Hill and then he:

Dash'd down to the Friars, where Romney's kind lord
Lives the friend of mankind, and's by thousands ador'd;
He again took the Medway, but faulter'd in pace,
While the old bridge at Aylesford befriended the chase:
At Hallong, sly Reynard had near met his doom,
Where Lambard the learned had chosen his tomb.

The fox is killed at Cobham. This song and other Kentish ballads were researched and recorded on LPs by Doug and Sue Hudson (a duo called 'Tundra').

A rich living tradition of Kentish singers and songs survived through the twentieth century featuring both local songs – such as the tragic 'The Constant Lovers', set at Fairlight – and local versions of more widely known songs. Many of the best mid-century singers of Kent songs also had strong links with Sussex, such as the East Sussex fisherman Johnny Doughty who sang 'The Wreck of the Northfleet', a nineteenth-century Kent broadside based on a Kent shipwreck, and George 'Pop' Maynard from Copthorne in Sussex, who annually went hop-picking in Kent, which he regarded as a 'holiday with pay', and where he learnt 'The Irish Hop-Pole Puller', an amusing song possibly of music-hall origin, of a laundry girl who deserts her coster boyfriend to run off with an Irish hop-pole puller:

I'm Coster Joe from down our street and me heart is nearly broke
I've lost me bloomin dona [girl], me coster cart and moke [donkey].
I'll tell you how it all occurred from the time we left the road
Till we got to the lovely fields of Kent.

CHORUS
For she was a modern laundry girl was blue-eyed Mary Fuller
Till she went and sloped from Kent with an Irish Hop-Pole Puller.

We'd started out from the Rose and Crown with mirth and pleasure bent
We caused a big sensation in every place we went,
For Mary Ann was well dressed up in a red-plaid shawl and hat,
And a lovely ostrich feather was bought by me the flat.

We started out for Crockham Hill and then for Hunton Bull
Oh Mary Ann expressly wished for to see 'em pick and pull
I loved her so I couldn't say no and we drove down to the fields
When suddenly the cart collapsed and off came both the wheels.

My Mary called, some fellows came, I could have done without 'em,
Especially two young Irish chaps with winning ways about 'em.
One said his name was Tim and the other Mick O'Brien,
Whom I could see with half an eye my Mary fixed her eye on.

Now I flew in a jealous rage and picked a row with Tim.
Mick O'Brien he picked it up and he knocked me in the bin.
And when at last the police came and hauled me off to jail,
It's wonder I'm alive here for to tell to you the tale.

And when I came out from doing time, I found myself forsook,
For Mary Ann and Tim O'Brien had slung their bloody hook,
So if you take your dona out don't take her down to Kent,
For you'll end up broke and you'll lose your moke and you'll wish you hadn't went.

George and Ron Spicer, well-known father and son singers and agricultural workers whose successive public singing careers span most of the second half of the century, both had that song in their repertoire. George came from Little Chart near Ashford, and both of his parents sang traditional songs. George learnt 'The Oyster Girl' and 'Searching For Young Lambs' from his mother Elizabeth (*née* Charles) and 'The Old Militia Drum' and 'Coming Home Late' from his father Richard. Another of George's songs, the risqué 'The German Clockmender' (or 'Clockwinder') is still sung by Alan Austen. George later moved with his family to Sussex; his son Ron became a favourite singer/accordionist at West Kent folk clubs where he often performed 'The Irish Hop Pole Puller' and another of his father's songs, 'The Folkestone Murder', a ballad based on the horrific murder of Caroline and Maria Black at Capel le Ferne in 1856:

Kind friends come pay attention, and listen to my song,
It is about a murder and it won't detain you long,
'Twas near the town of Folkestone this shocking deed was done,
Maria and sweet Caroline were murder'd by Switzerland John.

Ron also performed a memorable version of 'The Constant Lovers'. We have already mentioned Ken Thompson, a fine singer from Westerham who later managed a hop farm at Faversham and included in his repertoire (as well as the already cited 'Willie Taylor), 'Le Caffery' (his version of the infamous McCaffery army ballad), 'Twankydillo', 'The Mistletoe Bough', 'Shooting Goshens' Cocks Up' and perhaps the most popular of all hop-picking songs in the oral tradition (though rare in print) 'Hopping Down in Kent':

Now some says 'oppings lousy
I don't believe its true
We only goes an 'opping
To get a bob or two

Fred Cottenham, born in Fordcombe in 1923, was recorded by Mike Yates singing 'The Crockery Ware', 'Old King Cole' and 'Barbara Allen' in 1976, the former recording being featured on Mike Yates' 'The Horkey Load' cassettes for Veteran Tapes, which also included another fine Kent singer, Charlie Bridger of Stone in the Isle of Oxney, singing 'The Folkestone Murder', 'Three Maids a Milking Did Go' and 'The Zulu Wars'. Kent's rich tune heritage is represented by the Simons collection which contains a number of tunes names after hop-picking traditions.

Mike Yates has also researched the rich tradition of Traveller songs in Kent and Sussex, collecting material at the famous Yalding Horse Fair. His haul included Joe Jones singing 'John Barleycorn', Joe Cooper singing 'Ripest Apples' and Jasper Smith's version of 'The Hartlake Bridge Disaster', with its interesting corruption of 'Golders Green' for 'Golden Green' (which we have taken the liberty of amending in the version below):

> Now seven and thirty strangers, Oh a-hopping they had been;
> They were 'ployed by Mr Cox's only row, Golden Green
> It were in the parish of Hadlow, that's near old Tonbridge Town,
> But to hear the screams from those poor souls when they were going down.
>
> Now some were men and women and the others girls and boys.
> They kept in contact with the bridge till the horses they took shy.
> They kept in contact with the bridge till the horses they took shy,
> But to hear the screams from those poor souls as they were going down.
>
> Now some were men and women, the others girls and boys.
> They were 'ployed by Mr Cox's only row Golden Green.
> It was in the parish of Hadlow, that's near old Tonbridge town,
> But to hear the screams from those poor souls when they were going down.

At the start of the twenty-first century, the living tradition of Kent song is being kept alive by performers such as Andy Turner (who brought Charlie Bridger to the attention of the folk fraternity), Dave Watts, Tony Deane, John Morgan, Alan Austen, Chris Addison and Pete Castle, all of whom have strong links with these and other bygone Kent and Sussex singers whom they have seen and heard recordings of by field researchers such as Mike Yates, Ken Stubbs and Simon Evans. Mike and Simon in particular have recorded and drawn attention to the fine traveller tradition of singing in Kent, through records and radio documentaries. It is vital that folksong and music survives as a living tradition and not just in the archives and carefully researched new songs on traditional aspects of Kent life are being added to the live repertoire by singer-songwriters such as Bob Kenward, who writes of smugglers and the 'lookers' (shepherds) of Romney Marsh, the flint-knappers, fruit-growers, hoppers and hoodeners. Folksong is the DNA of Kentish traditional culture, a transmission of the essential and developing link between man and his working and living environments; its survival and continuance of development is vital.

NOTES & ACKNOWLEDGEMENTS

We wish to particularly thank Alan Austen, Tony Deane, Simon Evans, George Frampton, Anne Hughes, Mick Lynn, Richard Maylam, Glenn and Nick Miller, Roy Palmer, Doc Rowe, the late Ken Thompson, Dave Watts, Carl Willetts and Mike Yates for use of articles, information provided and discussions over the years and Hamish Mackay Miller for use of the excellent *Bygone Kent* series of magazines. We should also like to acknowledge use of the collections and the assistance of librarians/staff of: The British Library; the Centres For Kentish Studies at Maidstone and Strood; the Deal Maritime Museum; the Folklore Society Library; the Guildhall Museum at Sandwich; the Kent Archaeological Society Journals; the Reference Libraries of Folkstone, Maidstone, Rochester, Sevenoaks and Tonbridge (including use of the Tonbridge Free Press); The Templeman Library, University of Kent and The Vaughan Williams Memorial Library with its excellent librarian Malcolm Taylor.

For full details of works cited, see the bibliography.

Introduction

For information on Gavelkind see articles by C.L. Sinclair Williams, *The Codification of the Customs of Kent* and Percy Maylam *The Custom of Gavelkind in Kent* (thanks to Richard Maylam for providing this). For information on the Cinque Ports thanks to Sandwich Guild Hall Museum. Many of the proverbs are from Alan Major: *A New Dictionary of the Kent Dialect*.

Chapter One

For the folksong 'Dame Durden' see Bob Copper's *A Song For Every Season*; Thomas Hardy's *Far From the Madding Crowd* and the Hardy Family mss. A recording of the version by Bob and Ron Copper is available on their cassette *English Shepherd and Farming Songs* (Folk Legacy C-19).

For further information on Shrovetide see Fran and Geoff Doel and Tony Deane *Spring and Summer Customs in Sussex, Kent & Surrey* and *The Gentleman's Magazine*.

For May Garlands, Jack-in-the-Greens and Green Boughs see Roy Judge, *The Jack in the Green: A May Day Custom*; Fran and Geoff Doel and Tony Deane *Spring & Summer Customs in Sussex, Kent & Surrey*; Fran and Geoff Doel *The Green Man in Britain*; *A History of Bearsted & Thurnham* and Gilbert Hoole *A Tonbridge Miscellany*; plus articles – Thomas Trowsdale 'Garland Day in West Kent' and Edwin Harris's leaflet *Kentish Customs* and article *Recollections of Rochester*.

For Maidens' Garlands see *The Gentleman's Magazine* and *Plaxtol – a Kentish Village*.

For the account of Henry VIII and Catherine of Aragon's Maying see Fran and Geoff Doel *Robin Hood – Outlaw or Greenwood Myth*.

Our thanks to Mick Lynn for information on and photograph of Mr Jorrocks' Morris; and to Phil Burkin, Terry Heaslip and Nick Miller for information on Hartley morris; and to both morris teams for excellent dancing and welcoming sociability.

For Rogationtide and Beating the Bounds see William Lambarde *A Perambulation of Kent* and Fran and Geoff Doel and Tony Deane *Spring and Summer Customs in Sussex, Kent & Surrey*.

For Whitstable Oyster Fisheries and Grottos see A.O. Collard *The Oyster and Dredgers of Whitstable*; Robert Goodsall *A Third Kentish Patchwork* and Brian Day *A Chronicle of Folk Customs*. For Margate Grottos see Joan Rootes' article 'Only a Ha'penny Please'.

For gleaning see Brand *Observations on the Popular Antiquities of Great Britain* and *A History of Bearsted and Thurnham*.

For Charlton Horn Fair see broadsheets in the British Library collection cited (with illustrations) in E.P. Thompson *Customs in Common*. Thanks to Roy Palmer for providing photographs and details.

For 'The Horn Fair Song' see Tony Deane's research in *Spring & Summer Customs in Sussex, Kent & Surrey*.

Recordings are available by Sussex folksingers Bob Lewis on his cassette *A Sweet County Life* (Veteran Tapes VT 120) & Shirley Collins on the CD *The Etchingham Steam Band* (Fledgling Records FLED 3002).

Chapter Two

For Bonfire Night traditions see Dave Watts *The Edenbridge Bonfire Society*; *Plaxtol – A Kentish Village* and *A History of Bearsted & Thurnham*.

For Apple Wassailing see Hasted *History and Topographical Survey of the County of Kent*; Fran and Geoff Doel *A Kent Christmas*; Fran and Geoff Doel *Mumming, Howling and Hoodening: Midwinter Rituals in Sussex, Kent & Surrey* and Ronald Hutton *Stations of the Sun*.

For the Hooden Horse see Percy Maylam *The Kent Hooden Horse*; Fran and Geoff Doel *A Kent Christmas* and Fran and Geoff Doel: *Mumming, Howling & Hoodening: Midwinter Rituals in Sussex, Kent & Surrey*. Hooden Horses are on display at the Deal Maritime Museum and in storage at the Maidstone Museum. Thanks to Richard Maylam (great-nephew of Percy), Naomi Wiffen, Mark Lawson, Folkestone Library, the Deal Maritime Museum, the St Nicholas at Wade Hoodeners, the Whitstable Hoodeners and the Deal Hoodeners for valuable information.

For other Christmas and New Year superstitions and songs see Fran and Geoff Doel *A Kent Christmas*; Cecil Sharp's *Field Note Books* mss in the Vaughan Williams Memorial Library; the *Invicta Magazine* and *The Diaries of Lady Anne Clifford*.

Thanks to Simon Evans for the newspaper cutting giving the words of the Gravesend versions of 'The Seven Joys of Mary' and 'As I Sat on a Sunny Bank'.

Chapter Three

For smuggling see Mary Waugh: *Smuggling in Kent & Sussex 1700-1840*; Richard Barham *The Ingoldsby Legends* and Richard Platt *The Ordnance Survey Guide to Smugglers' Britain*.

For the Goodwin Sands see Parish and Shaw *A Dictionary of Kent Dialect* and Fran and Geoff Doel *A Kent Christmas*.

For Fishing Lore see Chaucer: 'The Prologue to the Cook's Tale' and The *Invicta Magazine*.

Chapter Four

Much of our information on hop farming in Kent comes from Ken Thompson's oral reminiscences of hop farming in the 1950s and early '60s when he managed a hop farm in Faversham. The account of Father Richard

Wilson's work in the hop gardens is taken from Miles Sargent 'The Day's Work' from *St Francis of the Hop Fields*, 1933. We are indebted to Mrs Anne Hughes who has generously permitted us to publish Alice Ransome's letter with her account of the Hartlake Bridge Disaster and the gipsy custom of throwing hop wreaths into the Medway.

Chapter Five

Information on the 'Light' of St Mary of Broadstairs comes from Archdeanery Court, vol. III, p.13. Details of the hermit of the chapel of St James, Reculver, comes from Edward Hasted, *History of Kent*, vol. iii, p.635, and on the medieval bridges the same author's *History of Strood, 1450*, pp.133-4. Information on the cult of St Blaise in Kent comes from C. Seymour, *Survey of Kent*, 1776

Chapter Six

For the record of the Lydd Passion play see Giles E. Dawson, *Records of Plays and Players in Kent, 1450-1642*, Collections, vol. VII, London, Malone Society, 1965, pp.89-112.

For Holinshed's account of the tragedy of Arden of Faversham see Holinshed, vol. IV, p.1024. For information on Kent Mummers Plays, particular thanks to Alan Austen, Simon Evans and Carl Willetts and thanks for details of and discussions on the Darenth Valley traditions to the late Charlie Jacob, Simon Evans, Terry Heaslip and Nick Miller. Thanks to the Folklore Society for access to the *Ordish Collection*. For printed sources see Alan Smith 'A West Kent Mummers Play'; Annis Cumfrey 'Kentish Mummers and morrismen'; Simon Evans 'The Darenth Valley Champions'; Carl Willetts 'Kent 'Seven Champions' and a Play From Milton Regis' and Fran and Geoff Doel: *Mumming, Howling & Hoodening: Midwinter Rituals in Sussex, Kent & Surrey*.

Chapter Seven

The letters referred to in the text are from *Letters and Papers, Foreign and Domestic, of the Reign of Henry VIII*, xviii (2), pp.296, 300. Reginald Scot's references to the practices of 'cunning men' come in *The Discoverie of Witchcraft*, vol. I, p.198. For the account of the 1610 'conjurors' see *Records of Maidstone*, Maidstone, 1926, pp.266-7. Some of the information on the Maid of Kent comes from Walter Jerrold, *Highways and Byways in Kent* (London, Macmillan, 1908). We do not necessarily agree with his conclusions.

Most of the witch trials are mentioned in C. L'Estrange Ewen's books (see bibliography), and Keith Thomas's book, but for the trial of Thomas Fansome, consult Kent R.O. PRC 44/3, pp. 167-8. For the 1653 trial, see Kent R.O. Q/SB/4, ff., 3-5.

Chapter Eight

For traditions of the invasions see Gildas *The Ruin of Britain*; Bede *Ecclesiastical History of the English People*; Geoffrey of Monmouth *History of the Kings of Britain*; Lambarde *Perambulation of Kent*; Camden's *Britannia* and Paul Ashbee's article 'Julliberrie's Grave, Chilham. Retrospection and Perception'. For monsters and spectral hounds see Charles Igglesden *Saunters in Kent* and R.B. Parish, *Animal Harbingers, Strange Creatures And Other-Worldly Beasts*. For legendary sayings see Parish and Shaw *A New Dictionary of Kent Dialect*. For ghosts see Richard Barham *The Ingoldsby Legends*; Peter Underwood *Ghosts of Kent*; Fran and Geoff Doel *A Kent Christmas* and *Plaxtol – A Kentish Village*. For information on Thomas Ingoldsby's use of landscape in his Kentish legends, see Charles G. Harper *The Ingoldsby County*.

Chapter Nine

For sale of wives see E.P. Thompson *Customs in Common*; George Frampton 'The Sale of a Wife' and the Tonbridge Civic Society Newsletter for Winter 1997. For poaching and poaching songs see Geoff and Fran Doel 'Ken Thompson – a Kentish Man and His Songs' – who recorded Ken's version of 'Willie Taylor' printed in this chapter. The Tonbridge example is from the *Tonbridge Free Press*. For highwaymen and footpads see *The Maidstone Journal* for 23 January 1787 and examples from the Canterbury press of 1770 quoted by Robert Goodsall in his *A Second Kentish Patchwork*. For skimmity riding and rough music see Thomas Hardy *The Mayor of Casterbridge*; E.P. Thompson *Customs in Common* and *The Weald of Kent*.

Chapter Ten

For The Biddenden Dole see Edward Hasted *The History & Topographical Survey of the County of Kent*; *The Story of Biddenden*; and Fran and Geoff Doel and Tony Deane *Spring and Summer Customs in Sussex, Kent and Surrey*. For St Nicholas's Hospital Harbledown see Rev Canon Derek Ingram Hill, *St Nicholas Harbledown*. For St Bartholomew's Hospital, Sandwich thanks to the Guild Hall Museum Sandwich. For the Watts Charity at Rochester see Charles Dickens, The Seven Poor Travellers. For Goodening see William Hone *The Every-Day Book* (1826 edition) and George Frampton 'Doleing For St Thomas'.

Chapter Eleven

Thanks to The Vaughan Williams Memorial Library and the Cecil Sharp Estate for quotes from the field notebooks of Cecil Sharp and other collectors. We have drawn substantially on *A Kentish Garland* for printed ballads and on recordings notes and articles by Mike Yates and Ken Stubbs, with supplementary help over the years from Alan Austen, Dick Richardson, Chris Addison, Dave Watts, Tony Deane, Mick Lynn, John Morgan and Andy Turner. 'Death and the Lady' (memorably performed by John Morgan) is found in *The Penguin Book of English Folk Song*. We have also drawn on our own recordings and experience of the folk music scene in Sussex and Kent over the past thirty-eight years.

Some recordings of Kent traditional singers can be found on The Horkey Load cassettes volumes I & II in the *Veteran Tapes* series (VT 108 & VT 109). A number of interesting traditional Kent songs by more recent singers (including Ron Spicer and Andy Turner) can be found on *The Keys of Canterbury* cassette (MATS 0010). A fine (augmented) version of James Beale's 'The Bold Fisherman' is found on Andy Turner's cassette *Love, Death and the Cossack* (AUD001), together with 'Deserter from Kent' (collected in Surrey). Ron Spicer's cassette *Following My Dear Old Dad* features 'Blackberry Fold' and 'Searching For Young Lambs For modern Kentish songs in the traditional idiom plus traditional Kentish tunes from the Simons family listen to Bob Kenward's CDs *Man of Kent* (COSOO5) and *The Straggling Bine* (AHS002). Excellent versions of 'The Watercress Girl' and 'Hopping Down in Kent' are found on Alan Austen's cassette *Songs For the Lady in White*.

APPENDIX

THE SHOREHAM MUMMERS PLAY

Enter FATHER CHRISTMAS

FATHER CHRISTMAS
In comes I, old Father Christmas,
Welcome or welcome not,
And I hope old Grandfather Christmas
Will never be forgot.
For in this room there shall be shown
The dreadfullest battle that ever was known.
So walk in St George, with thy free heart
To which claims peace in thine own part.

Enter ST GEORGE

ST GEORGE
In comes I, St George
That man of courage bold
With my long sword and spear
I won ten crowns of gold.
I fought the fiery dragon

And drove him to the slaughter
And by that means I won
The King of Egypt's daughter.
Any man that entereth that door,
I'll hack him small as dust
And send him to the cook shop
To be made into mince pie crust.

Enter TURKISH KNIGHT

In comes I, the Turkish Knight
From out of Turkey land to fight.
I'll fight with thee, St George, St George,
That man of courage bold,
And if your blood's too hot,
I'll quickly fetch it cold.

ST GEORGE
Ho, ho, my little fellow
Your talk is very bold
And just like these young Turks,
So I've been told.
Pull out your purse and pay,
Pull out your sword and spear
And we'll have satisfactory
Before thou goest away.

TURKISH KNIGHT
Satisfactory! There'll be no satisfactory at all!
My head is made of iron,
My body is lined with steel
And I'll fight with thee St George
To see which on the ground shall fall.

They fight

Enter BOLDSLASHER

BOLDSLASHER
In comes I, old Boldslasher
Boldslasher, with my long glittering sword and spear
I mean to part these two young men.

He parts them, but Turkish Knight falls wounded to the ground

ST GEORGE
O behold, what have I done?
I've slain my brother 'neath the evening sun!
Is there a doctor to be found
To cure this man lying bleeding on the ground?

Enter DOCTOR

DOCTOR
Yes, there's a doctor to be found
To cure this man lying bleeding on the ground.

ST GEORGE
What canst thou cure, Doctor?

DOCTOR
I can cure the ipsi pipsi and the gout
That's a pain runs neither in nor out,
Or a broken leg or a broken arm
I soon can cure the pain.
And if thou breakest thy neck
I can out and set it again.
I went five mile and a half last night
To cure an old woman of the toothache.
And how do you think I done it?
– Cut her head off and throw'd the rest
Part of her body in the dike –

ST GEORGE
What's your fees, Doctor?

DOCTOR
Twenty guineas is my fee
But I'll take ten pounds of thee!
I carry a little bottle in my inside pocket
Called 'allikan-pane'
I'll pour three drops on this man's nose
And he'll rise and fight again.

TURKISH KNIGHT is revived

TURKISH KNIGHT
O pardon me, St George
O pardon me I pray,
O pardon me this once
And I'll always be thy slave.

Enter QUINGQUANG

QUINQUANG
In comes I, little Quingquang,
Just come from the press gang
I'll press all on board a ship!!

Enter JOHNNY JACK

JOHNNY JACK
And my name is little Johnny Jack
With my wife and family at my back.

He turns and shows a large doll and several smaller ones tied to his back

Although I'm short and stout and small
I count myself best man amongst you all.
Roast beef, plum pudding, and mince pie
Who likes better than old Grandfather Christmas and I?
A jug of Christmas ale, sir.
'd make us merry and sing
And money in our pockets
'd be a very fine thing.
So ladies and gentlemen, there at your ease,
Give us Seven Champions, jut what you please.

Source note

Taken down by dictation from Mr W.J. Atkinson of Rolvenden, who took part in performances in the Sevenoaks area as a boy living in Shoreham in the 1890s. It was printed in an article in the *Kent County Journal* by Alan Smith entitled 'A West Kent Mummers' Play'.

Performance note

St George and the Turkish Knight were 'clothed in red soldiers' tunics'.

We have divided up the Quingquang speech to include a seventh character, Johnny Jack, as the second part of the Quingquang speech is elsewhere given by this seventh character. Usually Kent 'Champion Plays' are for seven parts ('The Seven Champions'), but (as with modern Mummers' sides) parts could be combined if the Mummers were one short.

BIBLIOGRAPHY

The following abbreviations are used:

AC: *Archaeologia Cantiana*
BK: *Bygone Kent*
EDS: *English Dance & Song*
R: *Roomer*
TA: *The Antiquary*

Paul Ashbee 'Juliberrie's Grave, Chilham, Retrospection and Perception,' *AC,* vol. CXVI, 1996.
Alan Austen 'A Christmas Tradition of the Frittenden Band' in *A Kent Christmas,* eds Geoff and Fran Doel (Stroud: Sutton, 1990, 1998)
Richard Barham *The Ingoldsby Legends* (Edinburgh: Bentley & Son, 1885)
Bearsted & Thurnham History Book Committee *A History of Bearsted and Thurnham* (Bearsted: Privately published, 1978, 1987)
Bede *Ecclesiastical History of the English People* (Harmonsdworth: Penguin, 1990)
Biddenden Local History Society *The Story of Biddenden* (Biddenden: 1980)
Alan Bignell *Kent Lore* (London: Robert Hale, 1983)
John Brand *Observations on the Popular Antiquities of Great Britain* (London: 1848-9)
William Bray (ed) *The Diary & Correspondence of John Evelyn* (Henry Colburn: 1854)

Camden *Britannia* (various editions, translations e.g. Holland, 1610, Gough, 1806)
Cawte, Helm & Peacock *English Ritual Drama* (London: Folk-Lore Society, 1967)
E.K. Chambers *The English Folk Play* (Oxford: Clarendon, 1933)
J.R. Chanter 'North Devon Customs', *Transactions Devon Assoc.*, ii (1867-68)
Geoffrey Chaucer 'The Parliament of Fowls', *Collected Works of Chaucer*, ed. F. Robinson (Oxford: OUP, 1970)
D.J.H. Clifford (ed.) *The Diaries of Lady Anne Clifford* (Stroud: Sutton, 1990)
A.O. Collard *The Oyster and Dredgers of Whitstable* (London: Joseph Collard, 1902)
Bob Copper *A Song For Every Season* (London: Heinemann, 1971)
Anthony Cronk *A Short History of West Malling* (West Malling: privately published, 1951)
Annis Cumfrey 'Kentish Mummers and morrismen' *BK*, vol. 9, no. 6
Brian Day *A Chronicle of Folk Customs* (London: Hamlyn, 1998)
Charles Dickens *The Pickwick Papers* (Harmondsworth: Penguin, 1972)
– 'The Seven Poor Travellers', *The Christmas Stories* (London: J.M. Dent, 1996)
Fran and Geoff Doel 'Ken Thompson – a Kentish Man and his Songs', *EDS*, summer, 1992
– *A Kent Christmas* (Stroud: Sutton, 1990, 1998)
– *Mumming, Howling & Hoodening: Midwinter Rituals in Sussex, Kent and Surrey* (Rainham: Meresborough, 1992)
– *The Green Man in Britain* (Stroud: Tempus, 2001)
– *Robin Hood – Outlaw or Greenwood Myth* (Stroud: Tempus, 2000)
Fran and Geoff Doel *The Hop Bin* (Stroud: The History Press, 2014)
Fran and Geoff Doel and Tony Deane *Spring & Summer Customs in Sussex, Kent & Surrey* (Rainham: Meresborough, 1995)
Fran and Geoff Doel and Terry Lloyd *Worlds of Arthur* (Stroud: Tempus, 1998)
Cecil Henry L'Estrange Ewen *Witchcraft and demonianism: a concise account derived from sworn depositions and confessions obtained in the courts of England and Wales* (London: Muller, 1970)
– *Witch hunting and witch trials. The indictments for witchcraft from the records of 1373 Assizes held for the Home Circuit, A.D. 1559-1736* (London: Kegan Paul, 1929)
Simon Evans 'The Darenth Valley Champions' ed. Geoff and Fran Doel, *A Kent Christmas* (Stroud: Sutton, 1990, 1998)
George Frampton 'Doleing for St Thomas', *BK*, 2000, vol. 21 no. 12
– 'The Sale of a Wife', *BK*, 2001, vol. 22 no. 12
James Frost *Animal Guising and the Kentish Hooden Horse* (Ozaro Books, 2023)
Richard Gem (ed.) *St Augustine's Abbey Canterbury* (London: Batsford, 1997)
Gildas *The Ruin of Britain* (Chichester: Phillimore, 1978)
George Gomme (ed.) *The Gentleman's Magazine Library* (London: Elliot Stock, 1883)
Robert Goodsall *A Second Kentish Patchwork* (Harrietsham: Stedehill, 1968)

Robert Goodsall *A Third Kentish Patchwork* (Harrietsham: Stedehill, 1970)
Francis Grose *A Classical Dictionary of the Vulgar Tonge* (2nd edition, 1788)
Thomas Hardy *Far From the Madding Crowd* (Harmondsworth: Penguin, 1874, 1978)
– *The Mayor of Casterbridge* (Harmondsworth: Penguin, 1886, 1978)
Charles G. Harper *The Ingoldsby Country* (London: Black, 1904)
Edwin Harris *Kentish Customs* (Rochester: Edwin Harris & Sons, 1899)
Edwin Harris 'Recollections of Rochester' series in *The Chatham, Rochester and Gillingham Observer*, 1932
J. Rendel Harris *The Origin & Meaning of Apple Cults* (Manchester: Manchester University Press and Longmans, 1917)
Edward Hasted *The History & Topographical Survey of the County of Kent* (Canterbury: EP Publishing, 1797-1801, 1972)
Revd Canon Derek Ingram Hill *St Nicholas Harbledown* undated
Christina Hole *English Shines and Sanctuaries* (London: Batsford, 1954)
Gilbert Hoole *A Tonbridge Miscellany* (Tonbridge: privately published for Tonbridge School, 1986)
William Hone *The Every-Day Book* (London: 1826)
Ronald Hutton *Stations of the Sun* (Oxford: Oxford University Press, 1996)
Charles Igglesden *Saunters Through Kent* (a series of over thirty booklets from the 1920s – bound copy available in Maidstone Reference Library)
Walter Jerrold *Highways and Byeways in Kent* (London: Macmillan, 1908)
Roy Judge *The Jack in the Green: A May Day Custom* (Cambridge: D.S. Brewer, 1979)
William Lambarde *Perambulation of Kent* (Bath: Adams & Dart, first published 1570)
Robert Latham and William Matthews (eds). *The Diary of Samuel Pepys* (London: Bell and Sons, 1976)
Sir Thomas Malory *Le Morte D'Arthur* (Oxford: OUP, 1998)
John B. Marsh *Hops and Hopping* (London: Simpkin, Marshall, Hamilton, Kent, 1892)
Percy Maylam *The Hooden Horse* (Canterbury: Cross & Jackman, 1909)
– 'The Custom of Gavelkind' (Canterbury, 1913)
Richard Maylam, Mick Lynn and Geoff Doel *The Kent Hooden Horse* (Stroud: The History Press, 2009)
Geoffrey of Monmouth *History of the Kings of Britain* (Harmondsworth: Penguin, 1966)
Thomas More *Dialogue Concerning Tyndale* vol. II (London and Lincoln: Eyre and Spottiswoode, 1931)
Frank Mundell *Stories of the Lifeboat* (London: published for 'The Sunday School Union', 1894)
Don Minifie 'May Day at Whitstable' *EDS*, Spring, 1978
Robert Neuman *The Plague House Papers* (Hutchinson, 1959)
George Orwell *A Clergyman's Daughter* (Harmondsworth: Penguin, 1964)
R.B. Parish 'Animal Harbingers, Strange Creatures And Other-Worldly Beasts' *BK*, 2001, vol. 22 no.12

Parish and Shaw (aug. Alan Major) *A New Dictionary of Kent Dialect* (Rainham: Meresborough, 1981)
Richard Platt *The Ordnance Survey Guide to Smugglers' Britain* (London: Cassell, 1991)
Plaxtol WI *Plaxtol – A Kentish Village* (Tonbridge: Tonbridge Free Press, 1957)
Joseph Ritson *Life of Robin Hood* (London: E.P. Publishing, 1795)
Joan Rootes 'Only a Ha'penny Please' *BK*, 1988, vol. 9 no. 12
Miles Sargent *St Francis of the Hop-Fields* (1933)
Reginald Scot *A Perfite Platform of a Hoppe Garden* (London: Henrie Denham, 1578)
Reginald Scot *The Discoverie of Witchcraft* ed. N.B. Brinsley (Elliott Stock: 1886)
Charles Seymour *A Topographical, Historical and commercial survey of the cities, towns and villages of Kent*
(Canterbury: privately printed, 1776-80)
Henry Smetham *History of Strood*
(Rochester: John Hallewell Publications, 1899, reprint 1978)
R. Skinner *A History of Bearsted School*
(Bearsted: privately printed, 1946)
C.L. Sinclair Williams 'The Codification of the Customs of Kent', *AC,* vol. XCV, 1979
Bob Tatman *The Hartley Morris Men 1952-1992* (Orpington: privately printed, 1992)
Keith Thomas *Religion and the Decline of Magic*
(Harmondsworth: Penguin, 1971)
E.P. Thompson *Customs in Common* (London: Merlin Press, 1991)
Tonbridge Civic Society Newsletter, Winter, 1997
Thomas Trowsdale 'Garland Day on West Kent', *TA*, June 1880
Peter Underwood *Ghosts of Kent* (Rainham: Meresborough, 1985)
Ralph Vaughan Williams & A.L. Lloyd *The Penguin Book of English Folk Songs*
(Harmondsworth: Penguin, 1959)
Julia de Vaynes (ed.) *The Kentish Garland* (2 vols) (Hertford: Austin, 1881, 1882)
Dave Watts 'The Edenbridge Bonfire Society', *Fireworks*, 1985
Mary Waugh *Smuggling in Kent & Sussex 1700-1840* (Newbury: Countyside Books, 1985)
Jennifer Westwood *Albion* (London: Grafton, 1985)
Carl Willetts 'Seven Champions and a Play from Milton Regis' *R*, 1985, vol. 5 no. 5

INDEX

Albinus, Abbot   102
apple wassailing   33-34
Archbishops:
   Augustine   67
   Alphege   79
   Ambrose   103
   Becket   72-74, 76, 77, 82-84, 107-108, 110, 124
   Cranmer   100;
   Lanfranc   73
   Warham   94
Arden, Thomas (of Faversham)   86
Arden of Faversham (play)   86
Armiger, Charles   133
Ashford   51
Aylesford   103-104
Aylesford Priory   79

Barham Down   104
Barham, Richard   49, 52, 110-112
barming, 127
Barton, Elizabeth (Holy Maid of Kent)   74, 99-100
Bearsted   17, 27, 32
Beating of the Bounds   23-25
Becket, Gilbert   107-108
Becket, murderers of   72-73

Bede, the Venerable   36, 67, 102-103
Bell and Jorrocks, the (public house)   22
Bethersden   93-94
Biddenden   42
Biddenden dole   16, 122-124
Bilsingham Priory   51, 109
Birchington   112
black dog legends   105-106
Blackheath   117-118
Black Horse, Pluckley   110
Black Prince, the   76, 108
Blacksmith customs   32-33, 69
Bleak House, Broadstairs   53
Blean   34
blessing the plough   46
blessing the sea   25
Bluebell Hill   103-104, 133
Bonfire Night   31-32
Boy Bishops   81-82
Brasted   43, 87
Brightlingsea   8
Broadstairs   53, 71
Broadstairs Folk Festival   129
Bromley   18, 48-49
Brookland   51, 115

Caesar, Julius 9, 102
Camden, William 69, 101
Canterbury 23, 40-42, 49, 53, 67, 69-70, 94, 110-111, 114, 119
Canterbury Cathedral 73, 76, 81-84, 108
Capel 117
Cardinal's Error, the (Tonbridge pub) 108
Catigern 103-104
Caxton, William 77
Chalk 49
Charlton 29
Charlton Horn Fair 27-29
Chatham 19
Chaucer, Geoffrey 13, 45, 56, 72-73, 117
Chequers Inn, Bickley 108
Chevening 43
Childes, William 94
Chilham 110
Chilham Castle 102
Chipstead 43
Chislet 36
Chittended, Silas ('Chittended Charity') Plaxtol 124
Christmas feasting 40
Christmas music and songs 42-44
Christmas, Puritan assault on 40-42
Christmas Sheaf, the 40
Christmas superstitions 42
Chulkhurst Charity, Elisa and Mary Chulkhurst see Biddenden Dole
Cinque Ports 8, 48, 53
Clifford, Lady Anne 45-46
club walking 25
Cobham 134
  (Christmas bread dole 128)
Cook, Nell 111
Coopers' Arms, Rochester 110
corn dolly 27
'Countless' Stones, the (little Kits Coty House) 104
Court-at-Street (Court-at-Strete) 74
Courts of Brotherhood and Guestling 8
Coxheath 25
Cranbrook 42, 114, 123
Culmer, Richard ('Blue Dick') 80

Dartford 23-24
Deal 20, 37-38, 42, 53, 55-56
Defoe, Daniel 53
Den and Strond (privileges of) 8
Deptford 18, 29
de Shurland, Sir Thomas 111
Devil (Old Nick etc.) 28, 69-70, 75, 77, 97, 106
Dickens, Charles 7, 53, 108-109, 125-126
doles see Chapter 10
Dover 8, 48-49, 51, 55-57, 105, 107
Dover Castle 104
Dymchurch 49, 52

Eastbridge Hospital, Canterbury 124
Easter traditions 16
Eastry 78
Edenbridge 31-32
Eleanor, Duchess of Gloucester 99
Eltham Palace 40
Erasmus, Desiderius 74

Fairlight 52, 134
Fansome, Thomas 94
Faversham 49, 53, 69, 135
Finglesham 115
fishing lore 56
flora 21
Flowering Day 22
Folkestone 25, 48-50, 57, 77-78
folk songs see Chapter 11
Ford, Agnes 85
Fordcombe 135
Fordwich 8, 33
friendly societies and benefit clubs 25
Frittenden 42

Gavelkind 10
Geoffrey of Monmouth 34, 36, 103
George and Dragon (Tonbidge pub) 113
ghosts 108-110
Gilchrist Anne 131
Gildas 102
Gillingham 24
gleaning 27
Godmersham Park 101
Godwin, Earl of Wessex 55

'gooding', 'goodening', 'mumping' and 'dawdlin'   127-128
Goodwin Sands   53, 55-56
Goudhurst   50
Gravesend   44, 57, 131
Greatstone (near Dungeness)   69
Greenwich   18, 21, 29, 45, 117, 133
Greenwich Geese (Greenwich Naval Hospital)   57
grottos   25-26

Hadley, Dan William   99
Hadlow   17, 65
Halden   94
Hallowe'en customs   32
Hall Place, Bexley   108
handbell ringing   39
Harbledown   73, 76
Hardy, Thomas   113, 119
Harris, Robert   94
Hartlake Bridge Tragedy   65-66, 136
harvest customs   27
harvest supper   64
Hasted, Edward   33-34, 122-123
Hawkhurst   48, 50
healing or holy wells   75-77:
  The Black Prince's Well, Harbledown   76
  St Blaise's Well, Bromley   76
  Becket's Well, Otford   76
  Becket's Well, Shorne Wood   76
  Becket's Well, Bapchild   76
  Becket's Well, near Wateringbury   76
  St Edith's Well, Kemsing   70
  St Eustace's Well, Withersdane   77
Hengist   34, 36, 102-103
Herne Bay   36, 47
Hever   25
Hever Castle   45, 108
highwaymen   117-118
hiring fair   31
Hoath   36
Holinshed, Ralph   86
holly-boy   15
Holy Maid of Kent see Elizabeth Barton
Hooden horse teams:
  Deal   37-39
  St Nicholas-at-Wade   37-39
  Sandling   39
  Tonbridge Mummers and Hoodeners   39
  Walmer   37
  Whitstable   39
  Wickhambreaux   39
Hooden horse traditions   34-39
hoppers' Hospital   62
hopping huts   61
hopping missions   62-63
hoppers' specials   60
hop picking and customs see Chapter 4
Horn Fair   27
Horsa   36, 102-103
Horsted   133
howling see apple wassailing
Hythe   8-9, 48, 51, 53, 114

Ide Hill, 43
Ingolsby legends, the   49, 52, 110-112
Invicta, legend of   104
ivy-girl   15, 27

Jack-in-the-Greens   16, 18-20
'Jack of Dover'   56
St John's Hospital, Canterbury   124-125
Juliberry's grave   101

Keats, John   123
Kemsing   70, 108
Kentish Ague   9
Kentish Cousins   7
Kentish Fire   11
Kentish Man see Man of Kent
kings and queens:
  Anne Boleyn   31, 45, 108
  Bertha   67
  Catherine of Aragon   21
  Charles II   20, 22, 25, 42
  Cnut   78
  Edgar   70
  Edgar of Kent   78
  Edward I   10
  Edward IV   40, 80
  Elizabeth I   21-23, 45, 84
  Ethelbert   67, 102
  George III   25
  Harold   55, 104, 106-107
  Henry II   72-73

Henry III 10
Henry IV 99
Henry V 69
Henry VIII 21, 71-73, 84, 93
Joan of Navarre 99
Louis VII 73
James I 32
John 29
Mary I 84
Richard I 73
William I 10, 56, 104
Keston 33
Kits Coty House 103-104
Knole Park 45

Laberius, Julius 101
Lambarde, William 10, 24, 34, 70, 74-79, 101, 103-105
Lawse, William 94
Leeds Castle 99, 127-128
legends see Chapter 8
Lent 15
Lewisham 18
Linton 127
Little Chart 59, 135
looker (shepherd) 9
loose 127
Lady Lovibund, the [check] (ghost ship) 56
Lydd 21, 54, 84-85
Lydd Passion Play 84
Lympe Castle 110

mackerel fishing 57
Maidstone 15, 22, 25, 49, 74, 94, 114-115
maiden's garlands 18
Man of Kent (Kentish Man) 8-9
Marden 114, 133
Margate 27, 49, 53
Marshside 39
Maundy Thursday 16
'May', the 85
May Day 16-17, 19, 21
May morning dew custom 20-21
May garlands 16, 19-20
Maylam, Percy 10, 36-39
Maypole dancing 17
Maypoles 20
May Queen 16-17
Maximilian, Emperor 69

Medway, River 25, 27, 49, 65, 72, 88
Michaelmas Day (old style) 31
Milton Regis 91
Minster 112
Monkton 37
More, Sir Thomas 74, 98
morris dancing: general 22
  East Kent 39
  Hartley Morris 22
  Motley Morris 20
  Mr Jorrocks 22
  Stansted Morris 22
  Wadard Morris 88
Mother Baker (white witch of New Romney) 96-97
Mummers' plays (see Chapter 6):
  Bearsted 90-91
  Brasted 87-88
  Dover 92
  Leigh 88
  Plaxtol 88
  Riverhead 87-88
  Milton Regis 91
  Rochester 89
  Shoreham play see Appendix, 87
  Sutton at-Hone 87-88
  West Malling 88-90, 92
  Yalding 89
Mummers' teams:
  Bishop Gundulph's 92
  Brasted Champions 88
  Brenchley Mummers 92
  Darenth Valley 87
  Champions 87-88
  Hartley Morris 92
  Tonbridge Mummers and Hoodeners 35, 92
  Shoreham Champions 88
  West Malling 92

Nennius 36, 102
New Romney 8, 21, 81-82, 85
New Year gifts 45
Newington-by-Sittingbourne 25
St Nicholas Hospital, Harbledown 124-125

Oak Apple Day 25
Old Clem's night effigies 32-33
Orpington 18
Ordish Collection 92

INDEX

Otford   76
Our Lady of Broadstairs   110
Our Lady of Court-at-Strete   74-75
Our Lady of the Rock   71
oyster-fishing customs   26

Pageant of St Thomas   82-84
pancake customs and recipe   15
Penshurst Place   45
Pepys, Samuel   14, 20-21
Pest House, Cranbrook   109
Pilgrim's Way, the   105
Pitt, William   53
Play of St George   85
Plaxtol   18, 32, 109
Pluckley   109-110
poaching   115-117
press gang, the   17, 54-55
Priory of St Sepulchre, Canterbury   83
proverbs   7-11, 46

Ramsgate   35, 49, 53
Reculver   49, 52, 71, 110
Reinwin (Rowena or Roxena)   34, 103
Restoration House, Rochester   109
Robin Hood   21, 85
Rochester   18-20, 23-25, 27, 72, 108
Rochester Castle   109
Rochester Cathedral   24, 74, 81
Rogationtide   23, 25, 33
Romney   9
Romney Marsh   9, 47, 51-53, 84, 111, 115, 129
Rotherhither   29
rough music   119
Rumball   57
Rye   9, 51

Saints (*see* Chapter 5):
  St Agatha   72
  St Appolline   72
  St Augustine   77
  St Bartholomew   75
  St Blaise   76
  St Clare   72
  St Clement   32
  St Crispin   69
  St Crispinian   69
  St Dunstan   69-70
  St Eanswyth   77-78
  St Edith   70
  St Ermenburga   78
  St George   69, 85
  St James   26
  St John   72
  St Job   72
  St Luke   27, 29
  St Roch   72
  St Simon Stock (Simon Angelus)   79
  St Mary (Virgin Mary)   68, 71-72, 74, 76
  St Mildred   78
  St Nicholas   71, 76, 81
  St Petronill   72
  St Romane   72
  St Rumbald or Rumwold   57
  St Thomas à Becket   72-73, 76-77, 82, 107-108
  St William of Perth   74
  St Valentine   13, 72
Sandgate   48
Sandwich   8, 21, 53, 56, 73
Sarre   8
Scot, Reginald   72, 94-96
Seven Champions Plays *see* Mummers' Plays
Seven Poor Travellers, The   108, 125
Sevenoaks   17, 43
Shakespeare, William   14, 27, 86, 108, 117
Sharp, Cecil   129-131
Sheppey, Isle of   112
Ship Inn, Dymchurch   52
Ship Money   8
Shipwright's Arms, the   110
Shoreham   87-88
Shorne, Sir John   75
Shooters Hill   21, 118
Shrovetide   15
skimmity riding   119
Sidney, Sir Philip   45
Sittingbourne   131
Skinners Company, the   22
Skull's Gate Farm   106
Smeeth   95
smugglers (notorious):
  Richard Joy   54
  Slippery Sam   54

Joss Snelling   54
smuggling *see* Chapter 3
smuggling gangs:
   Aldington   51-52
   Hawkhurst   49-51
   North Kent Gang   49
Snargate   52
Speldhurst   113
Spencer, Edmund   7
Staplehurst   46
St Augustine's Abbey,
   Canterbury   56
St Bartholomew's Hospital,
   Sandwich (dole, Bun Race
   and biscuit)   125
Stone   94, 136
Strood   24, 72, 77
St Thomas' Day   122
St Vincent's Day   46
Sundridge   43
Surtees, John   22
Sutton-at-Hone   87-88
Syn, Dr   52

Tenterden   35-36
Thanet, Isle of   9, 35-36, 37, 67, 77-78
Thompson, E.P.   113, 115
Thompson, Ken   39-40, 61-63, 116, 135
Thorndike, Russell   20, 52, 89
Tonbridge   22, 113-114
Tonbridge School   22
Trottiscliffe   105
Turpin, Dick   108
Tunbridge Wells   11, 15, 69

Upnor Castle   24

Valentine's Day customs   13-14
Vane, Sir Harry   109
Virgin of Broadstairs, the   71
Vortigern   34, 102-103
Vortimer   103

Walliford, Joan   98
Walmer   40
Waltham Abbey   106
Warehorne   52, 129
wassailing   34-35
Watts Charity, the   125-127
Westerham   131, 135

West Gallery music and choirs   42
Westgate on Sea   49
West Malling   11
Weyer, Johan   96
Whitstable   16, 18-19, 25-26, 49, 53
Wickham   33
wife sales   113-115
Williams, Vaughan   28, 131
Wilson, Father Richard   62-63
Wingham   38
'wise' women (white witches)   93
witchcraft *see* Chapter 7
witch's mark and familiar, the   98
Woden   36, 67
Wolfe, General   31, 131
Wolsey, Cardinal   108
Woolwich   33

Yalding   89, 136
Yalding Horse Fair   136

Zacharias   96

The destination for history
www.thehistorypress.co.uk